Miracles
are
Guaranteed

Also by Bill Ferguson

How to Heal a Painful Relationship:
And If Necessary, How To Part As Friends

Audio and Video Cassettes

How to Love Yourself

How to Have Love in Your Life

How to be Free of Guilt and Resentment

How to be Free of Upset and Stress

How to Create a Life That Works

How to Create Prosperity

How to Find Your Purpose

How to Experience Your Spirituality

Spirituality: Teachings from a World Beyond

How to Divorce as Friends

Miracles
are
Guaranteed

BILL FERGUSON

Return to the Heart
P.O. Box 54183
Houston, TX 77254

Cover design by Mark Gelotte

Edited by Michele Hegler

Library of Congress
Catalog Card Number: 91-091573

ISBN 1-878410-20-2

Made in the United States of America

This book is dedicated to
my wife and best friend, Diane.

CONTENTS

PART I

OPEN YOUR HEART

PART II

CLEAN UP YOUR LIFE

CONTENTS

PART III

CONNECT WITH
YOUR LIFE FORCE

LOVE

Love is by far the most important thing of all. It is the Golden Gate of Paradise. Pray for the understanding of love, and meditate on it daily. It casts out fear. It is the fulfilling of the law. It covers a multitude of sins. Love is absolutely invincible.

There is no difficulty that enough love will not conquer; no disease that enough love will not heal; no door that enough love will not open; no gulf that enough love will not bridge; no wall that enough love will not throw down; no sin that enough love will not redeem.

It makes no difference how deeply seated may be the trouble, how hopeless the outlook, how muddled the tangle, how great the mistake; a sufficient realization of love will dissolve it all. If only you could love enough you would be the happiest and most powerful being in the world.

— Emmet Fox

PART I

◆

OPEN YOUR HEART

When love is present, life works. You are happy, alive and free. Life is an adventure.

You once lived in this state of love, but then you got hurt and began closing down. You didn't know how to heal your hurt so you pushed your hurt inside.

As you avoided your hurt, you created fears and sabotaged your life.

As you heal your hurt, you set yourself free. You restore your love and your effectiveness in life.

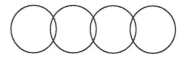

CHAPTER 1

CREATE THE
EXPERIENCE OF LOVE

Every aspect of life can be effortless, full of love and aliveness. This may seem impossible but it's not. This is actually the natural state. You lived this way when you were a young child, but you lost this state in the process of growing up. Now you can regain this joy for life. You can set yourself free inside and have your life be the exciting adventure it once was.

Happiness is what we seek, but we think that happiness comes from outside of ourselves. We then try to force and manipulate life to make us happy, never noticing that this doesn't work. In fact, the more we insist and demand how life should be, the more upset we become and the more our happiness eludes us. We create resistance against ourselves and repeatedly sabotage our dreams.

The key to having life be effortless is to find love and happiness within. Until you do this, your life will forever be uphill.

You gain this inner love and happiness by restoring the experience of love.

When the experience of love is present, life is a joy. You are happy and alive. You have an inner freedom and peace. You feel good about yourself, your life and everyone around you. You are confident and effective, full of energy and creativity.

You see life clearly and know what you need to do. You flow with whatever happens. Upsets and problems disappear. You become an expression of love and light up the world. Life works wonderfully and great things happen. This is the experience of love.

The experience of love seems to be a function of other people and what happens around you, but it isn't. The experience of love is a function of you. You create or destroy the experience of love by how you relate to life.

The best way to demonstrate this is by

looking at relationships.

Every time you interact with another person you either create love or destroy love. You create love by giving acceptance and appreciation. You destroy love by being non-accepting and critical.

Notice how you feel when someone genuinely accepts and appreciates you. Doesn't this feel great? Of course it does. You feel better about yourself and better about life. You also feel better about the other person.

The same thing happens when you accept and appreciate someone else. That person automatically feels better about life and better about you. By giving acceptance and appreciation, you create the experience of love.

Now notice how you feel when someone is non-accepting and critical toward you. Instantly, the experience of love disappears. You get hurt and upset. You put up your walls of protection and automatically resist the person who is non-accepting and critical toward you.

The same thing happens when you are non-accepting and critical of another. That person gets upset, puts up his or her walls of protection and becomes critical and resentful toward you. By being non-accepting and critical, you destroy the experience of love.

Every interaction you have with another person will either create love or destroy love, and whatever you give will come right back.

If you want to have love, acceptance and appreciation in your life, you have to give love, acceptance and appreciation.

Unfortunately, accepting people is often much easier said than done. Some people are very difficult to accept and appreciate.

We believe that people should be a certain way, and if someone doesn't fit our standards, we become non-accepting, and get upset. We think that if we just get upset enough, the other person will somehow get the hint and change into the way we want him or her to be. Unfortunately, life doesn't work this way.

How many times have you tried to change someone? Have you ever been successful in permanently changing someone into the way you wanted? Not likely.

How many times have you tried to change someone and the person got worse? This is much more likely. Just look at how you feel when someone tries to change you. How do you feel about changing? Not very interested are you?

Find someone in your life that you can't accept.

Notice that this person has a particular view of life and a particular way of behaving. Notice that this person is the way he or she is without any regard for how you feel about it.

When you can't be at peace with the way someone is, you lose the ability to effectively deal with your situation.

Notice what happens when you fight and resist the way someone is. Instantly, the experience of love disappears. You get upset and close down. You lose your aliveness and your peace of mind. Your ability to see gets clouded. You can't see what needs to be done, and whatever you do tends to make your situation worse.

You also communicate very clearly that the other person is not okay with you. That person then gets upset and becomes non-accepting and critical toward you. Then you get more upset and more critical toward the other person. Then the other person becomes more critical toward you.

You create a cycle of conflict: a cycle of resisting, attacking and withdrawing from each other. This cycle then goes on and on without either person ever noticing his or her part in the conflict. The suffering you experience can be horrendous.

Look at any relationship you have that doesn't work. If you are truthful, you will see that you are not accepting the way the other person is. That person is the way he or she is. You just don't like it.

By resisting the truth, you destroy the experience of love and create the cycle of conflict. You create your own opposition and suffering.

The same is true in every aspect of life. Whenever you resist, you close down inside and destroy the experience of love. You lose your effectiveness and sabotage your dreams. Any area of your life that doesn't work is an area where you are resisting.

Resisting is a state of mind and doesn't change a thing except inside you. To handle a situation you need action, not resisting. Resisting only destroys love and keeps you from seeing the action you need to take.

If you could somehow let go of your resisting and make peace with your circumstances, you would remain free inside and be able to see what needs to be done. You could then take the action necessary to effectively handle your situation. You could restore the experience of love and have your dreams come true.

So why do we resist?

We resist so we don't have to experience certain feelings and emotions that get reactivated by the circumstances. These feelings are hurt from the past and feelings of being inadequate and not good enough.

Until you heal this hurt from the past and set yourself free inside, you will continue to resist. You will destroy love and create a life of suffering. Life will be uphill and true happiness will forever elude you.

To have life be effortless, full of love and aliveness, you need to be free inside.

If you want, you can be free of your past. You can have life work for you instead of against you. You can be naturally effective. You can live in the experience of love. This book will show you how.

ACTION TO TAKE

◆ Recall a time when you had the experience of love. Notice what your life was like. Notice how free and alive you felt. Notice how you felt about yourself and the world around you.

◆ At any moment, your life is the way it is whether you like it or not. Notice what happens to the experience of love when you resist the way life is. Notice what happens to the experience of love when you are at peace and appreciate life.

◆ Notice how you have created or destroyed the experience of love in your life.

◆ Ask yourself these questions: Are you willing to have the experience of love in every aspect of life? Are you willing to have your life be effortless, full of love and aliveness?

◆ Make creating the experience of love the highest priority of your life. As you do this, everything else will handle itself. Use this book to learn how.

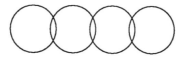

CHAPTER 2

HEAL THE HURT

The instant you get upset, the experience of love disappears. You close down inside and lose your ability to see what needs to be done.

Upsets seem to be caused by the circumstances, but they're not. No circumstance ever has the ability to make you upset. All a circumstance can do is strike a nerve in you. That's why the same thing can happen to two people and one will be upset and one won't.

If the circumstance caused the upset, then everyone, would react in exactly the same way. Obviously, this doesn't happen.

In one of our workshops we do an exercise that demonstrates this. We tell everyone to close their eyes and relax. Then we have them notice whatever feelings and emotions they experience when we say certain words. We say words like "you're fired," "I love you," "you can't do anything right," and "I don't love you anymore."

Each person has a totally different reaction to whatever words we say. When we say "you're fired," one person feels relieved and another feels devastated. When we tell them "I love you," one person feels warm and happy while another feels sad or afraid.

People react in different ways because each person has a different set of nerves and issues. These nerves and issues are suppressed hurt from the past and feelings of being inadequate and not good enough. We suppress this hurt and then spend the rest of our lives running from it. As we run from this hurt, we destroy the experience of love. We sabotage our relationships, our careers and our dreams.

To see some of the suppressed feelings and emotions in your life, notice what happens the instant you get upset. Instead of looking at your circumstances, look at what happens inside of you. Notice the immediate and powerful surge of feelings and emotions that come forth when you get upset.

Now notice how much you don't want to experience these feelings and emotions. Notice how you avoid or fight any circumstance that may reactivate this hurt from the past.

We think we are avoiding certain circumstances but we're not. We are avoiding the powerful feelings and emotions that these circumstances reactivate.

As we run from these feelings we create havoc in our lives. We automatically fight and resist any circumstance that may reactivate this hurt. We destroy the experience of love and make our lives much more difficult.

The more you are unwilling to experience these feelings, the more you have to run from them. The more you have to run from them, the more these feelings run your life.

If you could somehow separate your circumstances from your feelings and allow yourself to experience this hurt from the past, the feelings would lose their power and begin to go away. Avoiding these feelings gives them power. When you stop fighting them and make peace with them, they disappear.

This is what children do. When a young child gets hurt, the child cries. When the cry is over, the hurt is gone. Children are totally willing to experience their feelings. Allowing hurt is the natural process for releasing hurt.

We think that hurt is pain but this isn't true. Hurt is just hurt. Whether you experience hurt as pain or healing depends on whether you fight the hurt or allow the hurt.

Recall a time when you were hurt and allowed yourself to cry. Then, after you cried your last tear, you felt a wonderful freedom. Did you consider this hurt to be healing or painful? If you look, this hurt would be considered healing.

Now recall a time when you were hurt and hated it. How did you feel when you resisted your circumstances and fought your hurt? This hurt would be very painful.

When you are at peace with your hurt and are willing to experience the feelings of being inadequate and not good enough, the hurt loses its power and goes away. When you fight the hurt, the hurt becomes pain and seems to stay forever.

If you have a traumatic event in your past that still has power over you today, you have suppressed certain feelings and emotions from that event. To be free of this hurt, stop avoiding the hurt and face it. Be willing to experience all the feelings and emotions from what happened.

Go back in time to the moment the event happened and experience the event. Walk through the event step by step. Allow yourself to experience whatever emotions you have. Allow the hurt. When you get through, go back and do it again. Every time you walk through the event, you release more hurt. Do this over and over until all the hurt is gone.

Suppressed feelings and emotions also create addictions. We turn to cigarettes, drugs, alcohol, food, sex, work or anything else that may keep us from feeling this hurt from the past.

Instead of fighting your hurt, welcome your hurt. Do this so you can experience your hurt and be free of it. Hurt only does damage when you keep the hurt inside.

Be willing to experience anything.

Remember that whatever happens, you are only experiencing certain feelings and emotions from the past. That's all, just feelings and emotions. You can sit in your chair, experience any emotion and the emotion will soon be gone. When you know that an experience is only feelings and emotions, the circumstances are no big deal. When you see only the circumstances, you run into trouble.

Circumstances can be difficult to handle, but feelings are easy. So separate your feelings from the circumstances and be willing to experience whatever life has to offer. Experience your feelings and emotions, and let them go.

The next time you get upset, notice the feelings and emotions that you are having. Then notice that whatever you are feeling is totally separate from your circumstances.

As you separate the feelings from the circumstances and allow yourself to experience the feelings, you heal your hurt and set yourself free. The same circumstances can then happen again and you won't be as upset. Eventually, you won't be upset at all.

So take a look. Are there any feelings or emotions that you are unwilling to experience? Are you willing to experience failure or rejection? Are you willing to experience the loss of love? Any feeling or emotion that you are unwilling to experience will run your life.

If there is a feeling or emotion that you are unwilling to experience, notice that you experience that feeling all the time whether you are willing or not. In fact, the more you avoid experiencing these feelings, the more you bring them to you. If you avoid experiencing failure you will experience failure over and over.

Look at your upsets. Notice that the same feelings and emotions keep showing up. These feelings will continue to be reactivated as long as you avoid them. Whatever you avoid or resist will stay in your life until you finally make peace with it.

This is the beauty of the physical universe. Life will forever bring you the circumstances you need to discover and heal your hurt. Unfortunately we don't use life to find and heal our hurt. Instead, we run from our hurt. We run from the very circumstances that bring our healing.

To support your healing, create the declaration: "I am willing to experience anything." When this is your stand, you heal in the process of life. When you are willing to experience anything, there is nothing to fear and nothing can stop you.

The key to having life work is to be free inside and to do what works. When you are full of fear and upset you can't flow with life and you can't see what works. Being willing to experience anything will heal your hurt and set you free.

ACTION TO TAKE

◆ Notice what happens when you get upset. Instead of looking at the circumstances, notice what happens inside. Notice the powerful surge of feelings and emotions that get reactivated.

◆ Now notice how much you avoid these feelings and emotions Notice how you try to force life to be a particular way so you don't have to face this hurt from the past.

◆ Notice the damage you have caused by avoiding this suppressed hurt.

◆ Be like a young child and allow your hurt. Cry if you can. The key to healing your hurt is to make peace with your hurt. As you allow yourself to experience your hurt, your hurt disappears.

◆ Create a declaration that says, "I am willing to experience anything." When you are willing to experience anything, you heal in the process of life.

◆ Put your focus on healing the hurt instead of avoiding the hurt.

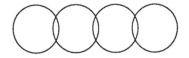

CHAPTER 3

LOVE YOURSELF

Each of us have several core issues that destroy love. These issues sabotage our relationships, our careers and our dreams. They destroy our aliveness and our peace of mind. They are the root of our hurt, our upsets and our self-sabotaging behavior. These issues are issues we have with ourselves.

When we were born, we were full expressions of love. Unfortunately, we were born into a culture that destroys love. As a result, we soon experienced a very painful, shocking loss of love from both our parents and our friends.

As a young child the only way we could explain this painful loss of love was to blame ourselves. Something was the matter with us. Why else would people treat us the way they do?

We decided that we were worthless, a failure, not good enough, or had some characteristic that kept us from being loved. This was the only explanation that made any sense at the time.

The loss of this love and the notion that we were not okay was so painful that we then spent the entire rest of our lives running from this hurt. We will do almost anything to avoid experiencing the feelings of being worthless or not good enough.

By avoiding these feelings we create havoc in our lives. We fight and resist anything that may reactivate this hurt from the past. We become defensive, full of fear and upset. We create turmoil and disharmony all around us. We do tremendous damage to our lives.

The irony is that the more you fight and resist these feelings of being not okay, the stronger they become and the more they run your life. When you run from failure, you create failure at every turn.

To heal this hurt and be free of your issues, you need to stop running from your hurt. Be willing to experience the aspect of you called not okay. Once you make peace with this aspect of you, there is nothing to run from. You heal your hurt and your issue disappears.

To discover and heal a core issue, take the following steps:

1. Discover as specifically as possible the characteristic you most avoid and resist.

2. Notice that this characteristic is just a point of view, a state of mind.

3. Accept that you are this way. Stop running from this aspect of you.

4. Notice that your being this way is "so what?" The same characteristic is in all of us and has nothing to do with what happens tomorrow.

Take the opportunity now to find and heal your core issue.

Find Your Issue

Your issue will be a characteristic that you can't stand. Just the thought that you might be this way will send cold chills up and down your spine. You won't like it at all.

To find your issue, find the characteristic that is most painful. Find the word or words that create the most discomfort. The more painful the words, the more damaging the issue.

Begin the process of discovering your issue by finding the word or words that you hate most to be called. What are the words that make you the most defensive or upset? Take a moment now and find the words.

How do you feel at the notion that these words accurately describe the way you are? If this notion is painful or if you deny that this is true, you are close to discovering your issue.

The notion wouldn't be painful and you wouldn't have to defend yourself unless the notion struck a nerve, and the notion wouldn't strike a nerve unless there was a nerve in you to be struck.

If someone said you are wearing a big yellow feather in your hair, you wouldn't be bothered a bit. If someone called you this unwanted name or characteristic, you would get upset. You wouldn't get upset unless down deep you believed the notion was true. By avoiding the feeling of being this way, you create your issue.

The following is a list of common core issues. Look them over and notice which words are most painful. If possible, have someone read them to you. Hearing an issue is usually more reactivating than reading one.

How do you feel at the notion that you are the following?:

unlovable	defective
not wanted	inferior
not needed	weak
not worth loving	helpless
worthless	subservient
no good	needy
not good enough	clingy
don't measure up	a wimp
inadequate	a coward
insufficient	lazy
less than	slow
useless	irresponsible
nothing	unreliable
unimportant	selfish
don't matter	dishonest
a nobody	bad
a loser	wrong
a failure	evil
can't cut it	heartless
don't have what it takes	miserable
incompetent	disgusting
screwed up	ugly
ignorant	fat

stupid   a scum
unstable   sorry
have something missing a slut

Notice that some of the words are painful and some aren't. The words that aren't painful are words you don't have an issue with.

Keep searching for the word or words that are most painful.

The characteristic you avoid is one you consider to be horrible. You decided that no one could possibly love and respect someone with this characteristic. As a result, you spend your life running from this characteristic, trying to become the opposite.

Someone running from the characteristic weak will do everything possible to be strong. Someone running from failure will do everything possible to be a success. Someone running from worthless will do everything possible to be worthy.

Unfortunately, you can never attain the characteristic you are driven toward. No matter how far east you go, you will still see west. Your issue will follow you wherever you go and whatever you do.

What characteristics are you driven toward?

Do you have to be a success? Do you have to be important, strong or worthy? Find the characteristic you are driven toward. Then look for the opposite. The opposite characteristic will be one of your issues.

These issues also create judgment. If you have an issue with failure, you will judge yourself and others by whether you are a success or a failure. If you have an issue with coward, you will judge on a scale called brave-coward.

Each of us has a number of standards by which we judge. We think that the whole world judges by the same standards, but the world doesn't. Each person has a different set of standards and each standard is created by a core issue.

What are the standards by which you judge? Find your standards and select the characteristics you feel are the most horrible. Find the characteristics you resist most in other people.

Any characteristic you can't stand in another person is actually a characteristic of yourself that you can't stand. You may not act like the other person, but that characteristic is still in you.

If you don't believe this, notice how you would feel if someone accused you of being just like the person you resist. You wouldn't like it. This would hurt. This wouldn't hurt unless you were avoiding the possibility that down deep, the accusation was true.

The moment you see that you are just like the other person, your resistance toward that person disappears and is replaced by compassion. Until you can see that the same characteristics are in you, your resistance will remain.

Any characteristic you resist, deny or find painful is an issue you have with yourself.

Although you may find many characteristics that are painful, select the one that hurts the most. Later, you will be able to work with all of them, but for now, select the one that is most painful.

Discover the Illusion

To say that you are a particular characteristic, or that you are not, is a little misleading. The truth is that you are just you and nothing more. Any judgment you add to this is just a point of view.

In fact, judgment isn't even real. Judgment only exists as a point of view.

For example, where can you find success or failure? You can't. Anything can be considered either a success or a failure depending on how you view it. Where can you find right or wrong? You can't. Right or wrong only exists as a point of view. Look at the chair you are sitting on. Is it good enough or not? One person would consider the chair good enough while another wouldn't.

To say that you are worthless is just a point of view. To say that you are worthy is also just another point of view. Neither are true. You are just you and nothing more.

The moment you decided you were worthless, or whatever your issue is, you created for yourself an illusion of worthy-worthless. You then ran from what you considered worthless to become what you considered worthy, all according to your point of view.

There are words on the list of common core issues that you don't have an issue with. Since you don't have an issue with these characteristics, you can't see them. You can't see them in you and you can't see them in another. You can only see characteristics that you have an issue with.

When you bought the notion that you were worthless, you bought an illusion and then spent the rest of your life running from something that doesn't exist.

Accept That You Are That Way

Although the characteristic you most resist is just an illusion, the hurt is very real. To heal the hurt, you have to stop running from the hurt.

The best way to heal this hurt is to make peace with the characteristic you resist. Accept that this characteristic is an aspect of you. Accept that you are this way whether you like it or not.

To say that you are this way is actually a lie, but as a point of view, this is the truth.

In fact, as a point of view, you are every characteristic that can be. You are both a success and a failure. You are strong and weak, worthy and worthless, right and wrong, good and bad. Every characteristic that can be, you are.

If there is any characteristic that you resist or deny being, you have an issue with it. This issue then runs your life. The more you avoid experiencing a particular characteristic, the more power you give to your issue and the more you sabotage your life.

To heal a core issue, you have to stop running from the characteristic and run toward it. Embrace that aspect of you. Own it. You don't have to like the characteristic and you don't have to express the characteristic. All you have to do is accept that this is an aspect of you. You are this way. You are many other ways, but you are this way too.

You may not show this characteristic all the time, but it's in you. Allow yourself to experience this aspect of you. Tell the truth. You are worthless, a failure, not good enough, and so on.

Forget that this is only an illusion and accept that this characteristic is a very real aspect of you.

Experiencing this aspect of you can be very uncomfortable, but this is what you need to do if you want to be free.

Review your life now and find all the evidence to prove that you are this way. There will be plenty of proof if you are willing to look. Just look at the times you have felt this way in the past.

If all you can see is evidence that you are not this way, you are only looking at one side of the coin. Notice how much you avoid this characteristic. Notice that down deep you are this way, pretending you are not. If this isn't true, why do you spend so much energy trying to be the opposite?

Feel the hurt associated with this issue. Notice all the times you felt this hurt in the past. Allow yourself to experience this hurt and let the hurt go.

Use the following questions to become more at peace with your avoided characteristic. Experience the hurt that gets reactivated. Work with each question until you can say "yes."

◆ Do you see how much you have avoided experiencing the hurt associated with your issue?

◆ Are you now willing to experience this hurt?

◆ Do you recall times in the past when you felt the hurt of being this way?

◆ Do you see the proof that you are this way? Look at the times you felt the hurt.

- Are you this way?

- Are you this way whether you like it or not?

- Are you willing to let yourself be this way?

- Are you willing to be this way forever?

- Are you willing to forever give up becoming the opposite?

- Are you willing to give up the opposite, and just be you?

- Do you feel a freedom in being able to just be you?

- Are you willing to love yourself just the way you are?

In surrendering to the truth, you set yourself free.

Keep letting in the hurt and the truth that you are this way. Don't fight it. Allow the hurt, and start moving toward "so what?"

So What?

So what if you are worthless, or whatever

your issue is? What difference does it make? None. What does it have to do with tomorrow? Nothing. You can still have your dreams. You can still have love. You can still have a wonderful, exciting, adventurous life.

The characteristic you've been avoiding has never caused you any trouble. All the trouble has been caused by your avoidance and resistance. The characteristic hasn't caused you trouble because the characteristic doesn't exist. The characteristic is only a point of view.

Once you accept that you are this way, and "so what?", the resistance disappears and you experience a wonderful peace. Your issue loses its power and you become free.

What a relief when you no longer have to be a success, worthy, good enough, important or whatever else you decided you had to be. Now you can just be you, and being you is all you need. In being you, you become free of the upset and become able to see what works.

Being able to see what works is the key to having your dreams come true. As long as you run from your issues, you won't be able to see what works. In fact, what works will be very irrelevant. The only thing that will be relevant is how to avoid experiencing your issues.

Healing your issues also allows you to make peace with you. Until you can accept every aspect of you, you will never be able to truly love yourself. How can you love yourself when you believe there is this dark, ugly dragon deep inside of you?

Accept yourself just the way you are, and allow yourself to be human. See the love and the beauty that you are, just the way you are.

Go through your life looking for core issues. Find them, heal them and set yourself free. Whenever you get upset, look for the issue that is being reactivated. Ask yourself, "What does that person or circumstance say about me that I don't like? What aspect of me am I avoiding?" Discover your issue, accept that you are this way, and "so what?"

The key to being able to flow with life is to love yourself. To love yourself, you must accept yourself. Accept every aspect of you, particularly the aspects of you that you don't like. Make peace with yourself so you can make peace with life.

ACTION TO TAKE

◆ Use the steps in this chapter to discover and heal your core issues. Find the aspects of you that you deny and resist. Then make peace with them. Remember, these aspects are part of you whether you like it or not.

◆ To love yourself, you have to accept yourself. Make peace with every aspect of you. See the beauty in your uniqueness.

◆ Give up having to be worthy, successful or good enough. Stop trying to be a particular way and allow yourself to be the way you are. Allow yourself to be human. Then go for your dreams.

◆ Notice the relief you feel when you give up having to be a particular way and allow yourself to be you. Notice how free you become when you heal a core issue.

◆ Go through your life looking for more core issues. Find them and heal them.

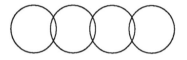

CHAPTER 4

BE WILLING FOR ANYTHING

To maintain the experience of love and to have life be miraculous, you need to be able to flow with whatever happens.

Often this is very difficult because certain circumstances reactivate a great deal of hurt and feelings of being not okay. You don't want to experience these feelings, so you fight and resist any circumstance that may reactivate them.

The moment this happens, you get upset. You stop flowing with life and close down inside. You lose the experience of love and your ability to see what needs to be done. Usually you make your situation much worse.

By avoiding these feelings and resisting your circumstances, you destroy love and create a life of suffering.

To restore the experience of love and to have a life that works, you need to be free inside. Stop fighting your circumstances and make peace with them. Make peace with the truth. Then do whatever you need to do.

The best way to make peace with a circumstance is through a process called letting go.

Letting go is giving up your demand for how life should be and surrendering to the truth of how your life is. Letting go is giving your circumstances full permission to be in your life. You don't have to like your circumstances, just give them permission to be there.

For example, JoAnne was about to lose her job and was full of fear. When I told her to be willing to lose her job she became very upset. "What do you mean lose my job? I have four kids and no place to go." She was terrified just at the thought.

The next day JoAnne came back and said she cried for hours and was now willing to lose her job. She didn't want to lose her job, but she was willing. She said, "Our family has been through tough times before and we survived them all. We'll survive this one too." Her face was noticeably relaxed. Her fear and panic were gone.

In her willingness to lose her job, she set herself free. She later reported that with the fear gone, she was able to produce ten times as much with one tenth the effort. By being willing to lose her job, she was able to keep it.

Letting go is giving up your demand for how you want your life to be, and making peace with the way your life is.

To let go, you have to be willing to experience all the hurt and feelings of being not okay that your circumstances reactivate.

Once you are willing to experience this hurt from the past, you no longer need to avoid and resist your circumstances. You can let go and make peace with your life. You heal your hurt and set yourself free.

You also see your situation very differently. You see solutions you could never see before. You restore the experience of love and become naturally effective. To demonstrate this in your life, select a fear you want to be free of. Do this now.

Fear is created by avoiding and resisting a future possible event. The more you avoid and resist this possible event or circumstance, the greater your fear.

What is the possible event or circumstance that you fear? What feelings and emotions would you have to experience if your fear were to happen? What aspect of yourself would you have to face? Be as specific as possible.

Are you now willing to experience these feelings?

To be willing, all you have to do is say, "Yes, I am willing." Being willing is just a choice. You don't have to like it, just be willing.

If you are not willing, notice that you experience these same feelings anyway, whether you are willing or not. So you might as well stop fighting your feelings and make peace with them. Be like a young child. Allow yourself to feel the hurt and emotion. As you do this, the feelings lose their power and go away.

The next step is to be willing for your fear to happen. A powerful way to do this is to tell God, "I am willing for my fear to happen. I give you full permission to bring it to me."

Say this and be willing to experience all the feelings and emotions that get reactivated. Say this over and over again until you can say this and mean it.

Once you are willing for your fear to happen, there is nothing to fear. You become free inside and able to see what needs to be done. You can then take whatever action you need to handle your situation.

Now go through your life and list all your fears. Work with each fear until you are willing for the fear to happen. As you do this, you heal your hurt.

Until you heal this hurt, the feelings and emotions you avoid will continue to be reactivated. Fear and upsets will appear over and over again. To have a life that works, find and heal the hurt that runs your life.

Another way to find suppressed hurt is to look for anything you are not willing to lose tomorrow. Are you unwilling to lose your relationships, your children or your job? Are you unwilling to lose your security, your money or your home?

Whenever you intensely avoid losing something, there is a hurt you don't want to experience.

For example, John and Kathy were in the process of separating. John didn't want to lose Kathy so he hung on to her. He thought he hung on because he loved her, but this wasn't true. If he loved her, John would want Kathy to be happy even if it meant losing her.

John hung on to Kathy because he didn't want to experience all the feelings and emotion he would have to experience if Kathy were to go. He didn't want to experience the hurt and the feelings of being not good enough. To avoid these feelings, John hung on.

The irony is that the more John hung on, the more he pushed Kathy away. Eventually he lost her. This is the way life works.

The more you avoid your hurt, the more you create circumstances to reactivate your hurt. In other words, whatever you avoid and resist will keep coming to you until you finally heal the hurt in you. Once you heal your hurt, you no longer need the avoided circumstances, and you become free.

If there is any circumstance that you can't be at peace with, there is a nerve that is being struck, a hurt that needs to be healed.

So look over your life. What circumstances

can't you be at peace with? What are you unwilling to have happen? What are you unwilling to lose tomorrow? What are you unwilling to experience?

Look for any area of life for which you are not willing. Then notice how irrelevant your unwillingness is. Your unwillingness certainly doesn't stop your fears from happening or keep you from losing what you don't want to lose.

Make a list of any circumstance that you can't be at peace with. Then work with your list until you are willing for each circumstance to be in your life. Let go and set yourself free inside. Then do whatever you need to do.

To let go and make peace with your circumstances, take the following steps:

1. Find the specific circumstances you are avoiding or resisting.

2. Find the hurt, the emotion and the feelings of being not okay that you don't want to experience.

3. Be willing to experience these feelings.

4. Give the circumstances permission to be

in your life.

5. Take whatever action you need to take.

Work with each item on your list until you are totally willing to experience anything life has to offer.

Remember that being willing is just a state of mind, and that your actions are totally separate. Being willing is the process that allows you to be free of the fear and upset that keep you from seeing what needs to be done.

The more you let go and make peace with your life, the more you can create a life that works.

Sometimes the process of letting go can seem very difficult. You can make the process much easier by trusting.

Trust that you will be okay no matter what happens. When you know that you will be okay, you have nothing to fear and letting go becomes relatively easy. When you don't trust that you will be okay, circumstances become threatening and letting go can be very difficult.

Trust is something you create. Trust is a choice, a declaration. "I will be okay no matter what happens. I trust, just because I say so."

The more you trust, the more you let go and the more your life works.

Trusting is also telling the truth. You really will be fine no matter what happens. Life is only threatening when you resist.

Look at your life. Have you ever had a situation you didn't survive? Of course not. You have survived everything. Tough times have only been tough because you resisted your circumstances.

So stop resisting. Be willing to let go of your life and trust. Trust, knowing that whatever happens is for your highest good. Trust that you will be fine.

Here is a prayer that is very powerful.

"God, I give you my life, my heart and my soul. I give you my relationships, my property and my health. You can take them all forever. Whatever you have planned for me is fine. I totally trust you."

To be totally willing for anything, you have to let go of your life, but once you do, you gain a life that will exceed your dreams.

Life becomes miraculous. Fear and upsets begin to disappear. You stop creating resistance and opposition against yourself. You live in harmony with the world around you, and life becomes effortless. You express love and receive love in return. You enter the garden of Eden.

When you are willing to lose your life, the only change is inside you. Everything you enjoy is still there. Only now you can appreciate your life like never before. When you are willing to have nothing, you become very thankful and appreciative for everything you have, and you have a lot.

Learning to let go and make peace with your life is a major step toward being free inside and having a life that works.

ACTION TO TAKE

◆ Make a list of every fear you have and then be willing for each fear to happen. Make a list of everything you are not willing to lose tomorrow and then be willing to lose it all. Make a list of anything else for which you are not willing, and then be willing.

◆ If you have difficulty letting something go, notice what you would have to experience if the circumstances you avoid were to happen. Then be willing to experience whatever you have been avoiding. Work with your lists until you are willing for anything.

◆ Trust that no matter what happens, you will be fine. When you trust, letting go becomes much easier. Trust, just because you say so.

◆ Go through your life being willing to experience whatever life has to offer. This will free you of the circumstances and allow you to gain strength and happiness from within. You will then become very effective.

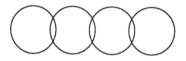

CHAPTER 5

EXPRESS YOUR LOVE

Love is the joy of life. When you feel loved, life is wonderful. You feel better about yourself and everything around you. You also feel better about the people who love, accept and appreciate you.

When you feel loved you naturally return love. So does everyone else. Watch what happens when you compliment someone or say how much you appreciate someone. Notice how happy the person becomes. Watch as the person fills with love and returns love to you.

To have love in your life, you have to open your heart and give love. As you give love, you receive love in return.

Unfortunately, expressing love is often a very scary thing. We are afraid that if we open our hearts and express our love, we will get hurt.

Several years ago we did a workshop for a group of nine-year-old girl scouts. As soon as we talked about expressing love to their friends, the girls became very uncomfortable. All of a sudden they wanted to stop the workshop and go out and play. As we talked with the girls individually, each girl said that she loved her friends but was afraid to let them know. "If I let them know how much I love them, they'll laugh at me, make fun of me and won't love me anymore."

By age nine the girls had already learned one of our culture's primary rules about love: If you don't want to get hurt, don't express your love.

We have all have been hurt and it's no fun. To make sure we don't get hurt again, we make decisions about what we should do in the future. We make decisions like, "I'll never open my heart again. Don't let anyone get too close. Don't express how you feel."

These decisions create distance and destroy love. We protect ourselves by pushing people away and holding ourselves back.

What decisions have you made to make sure you don't get hurt again?

To avoid experiencing the loss of love, we push love away. We deny ourselves the love we want so much. We want people to love us, but we make this very difficult.

Notice how you feel when you are around someone who is hard and protective? Notice how uncomfortable you feel. You don't feel loved and you certainly don't feel like opening your heart and expressing love.

Now notice how you feel when you are around someone who is very open, with little or no walls of protection. Young children are like this. Notice how this type of person pulls love out of you. Notice how loved you feel.

If you want people to be open and loving around you, you need to be open and loving around them. People react just like you.

We put up walls to protect ourselves from hurt, but the hurt we avoid isn't outside ourselves. The hurt we avoid is inside.

Look at the fear of opening your heart, being vulnerable and expressing your love. Just the thought reactivates old hurt.

A young child doesn't fear being hurt because the child has no hurt inside to run from. When the child feels hurt, the child cries and the hurt goes away. There is nothing for the child to fear. Only when you avoid hurt is there something to fear.

Walls don't protect us either. Walls only create opposition, destroy love and produce more hurt.

Your most powerful protection comes when you open your heart and are willing to express your love. Love melts opposition, creates harmony and heals hurt.

As you open your heart and express your love, you create life.

Look in the face of someone who is open, loving and unprotecting. What do you see? This type of person is alive. The person has happiness, freedom, inner peace and a joy for living.

All the words you use to describe this type of person are exactly the same words that describe the experience of love. The words are the same because what you see in an open, unprotecting person is love.

Love is the essence of who you are. Love is

your life force. When you allow love to come forth, you have life. When you cut it off, you have death.

Look in the face of someone who is very protective and unwilling to be hurt. What do you see? This type of person is rigid and dead. There is a thick crust of hardness, anger and resentment, and, beyond that, a tremendous amount of fear and suppressed hurt.

Which face would you rather have? Which life would you rather live?

To open your heart and be an expression of love, you have to be like a young child. You have to be willing to be hurt.

This doesn't mean go get hurt. You may need to say, "No." You may need to take action. Just don't run from your hurt. Be willing to experience any hurt that may come along. Make peace with your hurt. Cry like a child, and let the hurt go.

Remember, the hurt you avoid is only hurt from the past that you have suppressed. Every time you feel hurt, you have an opportunity to heal a little more.

Look forward to opportunities that allow

you to release more hurt.

The more you are willing to be hurt, the more you won't be. As long as you avoid hurt you will create hurt over and over again.

Here are a number of questions that can walk you through the process of opening your heart. Work with each question until you can say "yes" and mean it. Allow yourself to experience all the fear and hurt that gets reactivated by these questions.

◆ Are you willing to experience all your hurt?

◆ Are you willing to be hurt, again and again?

◆ Are you willing to let go of your walls of protection?

◆ Are you willing to be unprotecting like a young child?

◆ Are you willing to express your love?

The more you open your heart and express your love, the more you make it safe for people around you to do the same.

The world doesn't need changing; the world needs loving. There are five billion people on the planet and most all of them are afraid to open their hearts and express their love.

We go through life with our walls up waiting for others to take the first step and express their love. Then, if we feel safe enough, we will open our hearts and express our love.

Unfortunately, almost everyone is waiting for someone else to take the first step, and few do. As a result, we live in a world where people go around protecting themselves instead of expressing their love.

When your life is about opening your heart and taking the first step, you alter the planet. You make it safe for others to open their hearts and express their love. When enough people are willing to open their hearts and express their love, the rest of the world will follow. We will have a planet that is loving and supportive.

The process begins with you.

ACTION TO TAKE

◆ Take a stand on opening your heart and expressing your love. This may take courage, but as you take a stand on love, you literally alter the planet. You make it safe for everyone around you to express their love as well.

◆ Allow yourself to be open and unprotecting like a young child. Allow yourself to discover that the greatest protection comes from love, not walls.

◆ Be willing to be hurt again and again. Experience your hurt and let the hurt go. Once you are willing to be hurt, you no longer need your walls of protection. You naturally become an expression of love.

PART II

◆

CLEAN UP YOUR LIFE

The opportunity of life is to create and maintain the experience of love.

When you are faced with something in your life that doesn't work, the experience of love disappears. You close down inside. You lose your love, your aliveness and your peace of mind.

Every aspect of your life that doesn't work is a function of you. Once you discover this, you can begin to create a life that works, a life of freedom and peace.

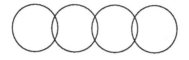

CHAPTER 6

WATCH HOW YOU SPEAK

When you were born, you were a full expression of love, but you knew nothing about the physical universe. You then began the exciting adventure of discovering life.

As life unfolded, you made decisions about the way life is. You made decisions like, "I'm creative" and "I like myself." You also made decisions like "relationships don't work" and "life is hard."

You thought you were discovering the truth of life, but you weren't. You were only deciding the truth for you.

These decisions, or points of view, then became like a computer program. They determined how you view life and how you interact with the world around you. You automatically act consistent with the way you "know" life is.

Your life then becomes consistent with your points of view.

If you know that relationships don't work, you will quit when the going gets tough. Why bother to put out the effort when you know that relationships don't work anyway?

If you know that life is hard, you will expect effort and struggle. You won't have the ability or the desire to take the action necessary to have life be effortless.

Likewise, if you know that you like yourself, you will seldom invalidate or criticize yourself. You will speak well of yourself and then like yourself even more.

As life proves your points of view to be correct, you become more and more convinced that you know the truth of life. This keeps you from discovering that your life is your own creation.

You create your life by the points of view you adopt. Some points of view forward you. Others do tremendous damage.

To have life be as wonderful as possible, create a reality that supports you. Keep the points of view that forward you and release the ones that don't.

What are the points of view that sabotage your life?

What have you decided is the truth about relationships, about love, about life? What is the truth about you?

Core issues are points of view. When you first experienced the loss of love and decided you weren't okay, you created a point of view. You then spend the rest of your life resisting your own point of view.

List every negative point of view you can find.

Here are some examples: "I can't handle money. Relationships don't last. I'm not good enough. I hate to exercise. You can't trust a man, or a woman. You have to fight to survive. Life is hard."

To release a negative point of view, all you have to do is say, "This is no longer true for me. I let go of this point of view." Say this and mean it.

Sometimes this is much easier said than done. Sometimes we don't want to let go of a point of view. This is true even when the point of view clearly sabotages us.

We hang on to certain points of view like we hang on to people. We hang on to protect ourselves. We hang on so we don't have to face something inside ourselves.

What negative points of view do you hang on to?

If you have resistance to releasing a negative point of view, find what the resistance is. What would you have to confront or experience if you could no longer have the point of view?

What is the hurt, the feelings or emotions that you are avoiding? What do you fear will happen? What will you have to face? What will you have to be responsible for? What will you have to confront about yourself?

Here are the steps to release a negative point of view.

1. Find the specific wording of your point of view. Keep the wording simple.

2. Notice that your point of view is not the

"truth of the universe," just your truth.

3. Notice if you have any resistance to letting it go.

4. If you have resistance, find what the specific resistance is. What are you avoiding by hanging on to your negative point of view?

5. Work with each item of resistance until the resistance is gone.

6. Let go of the point of view. Say to yourself, "This is no longer the truth for me. I let the point of view go."

7. Find a replacement point of view that will forward you in your life.

Continue to work with your negative points of view until you are free of every one of them.

Then go through your life searching for more. The best way to do this is to listen to your conversations. When you talk, your negative points of view will slip out. Whenever you make a statement that says life is a particular way, remember that this is just your point of view. If the point of view forwards you, keep it. If the point of view sabotages you, let it go.

Let go of all the negative points of view you have, and don't create new ones.

Be particularly careful when you are upset. Most negative points of view are created in moments of an upset. When you are upset, you relate very negatively to your situation. The points of view you adopt in an upset will almost always sabotage you.

When you get upset, instead of making another negative decision, like "Robert is a jerk," say something like this, "Robert seems to be a jerk, but I'm upset and I don't know for sure."

Also, be very careful how you speak. The more you speak negatively about something, the more that negative statement becomes your point of view. That area of your life then becomes consistent with the way you say it is.

Look at the areas of your life that don't work and notice how you speak about them. You speak very negatively. You speak your unworkability into existence.

When you speak negatively about something, you lose your power. You convince yourself that you have nothing to do with the problem. You put yourself at the effect of your situation and lose your ability to take action.

So don't speak negatively about anything. Don't speak negatively about yourself, about others or about your life, unless you want what you say to be true.

Every word you say is a prayer.

We go through life saying, "I don't have any, I don't have any, I don't have any." Then we stop and pray, asking, "Please, God, send me some." Then we go on saying, "I don't have any, I don't have any," and we wonder why our prayers don't get answered.

Well, our prayers do get answered. We're just careless about the way we pray.

If you want to be free of negativity and have your life work, stop speaking negatively. If something negative slips out, say "cancel that."

You also create by your thoughts.

Thoughts seem to be statements of truth, or fact, but they are not. Thoughts are just points of view, and have no power unless you believe them.

In one of our workshops we had people close their eyes and re-experience a past upset. While they were experiencing their upset we had them notice all their thoughts and write them down. When the exercise was over, we had them look at their list of thoughts and notice if the thoughts were statements of fact or just points of view.

When they read their list, they discovered that almost every thought was just a point of view. Although the thoughts seemed true at the time, they weren't. The thoughts were only points of view. The participants also discovered that many of these points of view were still running their lives.

You may never be able to stop your thoughts, but you certainly can determine which thoughts you accept. If you have a negative thought, let the thought pass on by. A thought has no power unless you grab on to it and believe it.

When you stop accepting negative thoughts, you stop having them.

The type of thoughts you receive are the type of thoughts you listen to. When you stop buying a particular type of thought, that type of thought stops showing up.

If you want to stop having self-invalidating thoughts, stop speaking negatively about yourself and stop accepting self-invalidating thoughts.

Don't buy any negative thoughts about yourself, about others or about your life.

Sometimes a situation can seem so bad that speaking positively seems like a lie, but it's not. There is beauty and opportunity in everything if you are willing to look.

Mary was a senior editor for a major news-paper until she lost the use of her hands in an illness. For her, this was very threatening. She not only had· to give up her job but her career as well. She didn't know what to do and became very upset.

Mary was then asked to find the opportu-nity of her situation. At first this seemed absurd. There didn't seem to be any oppor-tunity, but Mary kept looking. Finally, she found the opportunity.

Mary had always wanted to be a guidance counselor but couldn't. She was so involved in her career that she didn't have time. Now Mary saw that she could. She could go back to school, get her counseling credentials and do what she always wanted. The moment

Mary saw the opportunity in her situation, she became thrilled.

Mary's circumstances remained the same, but her point of view became very different, and so did her life.

Any situation can be viewed as either a predicament or an opportunity. Either one is just a point of view, but the one you choose is the one you get.

So watch what you say. You create your life by the way you say life is. If you want to have life be great, don't speak negatively. Look for the beauty and opportunity in everything.

ACTION TO TAKE

◆ Make a list of every negative point of view you can find. Then release each one. If you have resistance to releasing a negative point of view, work with the resistance until there is no more.

◆ Core issues are negative points of view. If you have resistance to healing a core issue, look for what you are avoiding. What would you have to confront or be responsible for if you lost your issue?

◆ Make sure you don't create new sabotaging points of view. Be particularly careful when you are upset. Let your thoughts have their say and let them go. Don't buy a negative thought unless you want the thought to come true.

◆ Watch how you speak. Don't allow yourself to speak negatively about your life, another person or yourself. If you say something negative, say "cancel that."

◆ Whenever you are in a tough situation, find the opportunity.

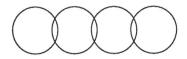

CHAPTER 7

LIVE AT CAUSE

At any moment, you are totally, one-hundred per cent at the effect of the world around you. Whatever happens around you, you will in some way react.

At the same time, the world around you is totally, one-hundred per cent at the effect of you. Whatever you do, the world around you will in some way react to you. This makes you cause.

You are totally at the effect of everything around you. You are also totally cause of everything around you. You are both cause and effect at the same time.

Although you are both cause and effect,

you only experience yourself as being one or the other. You either experience yourself as being the cause of your life or you experience yourself as being at the effect of your life. How you experience yourself at any moment determines your ability to deal with life.

When you experience yourself as being at the effect, your ability to deal with life becomes greatly reduced. Your situation seems bigger than you. You become upset and close down inside. You feel powerless.

When you remain at the effect, you close down even more. You feel defeated and want to cry. You lose both your confidence and your energy. You withdraw from life and become ineffective. Life then gets worse and you become even more at the effect.

When you are at the effect, all you can see are your circumstances. You don't notice that being at the effect is just a choice, a state of mind.

At any moment you have the ability to shift from effect to cause. You do this by generating a commitment and determination to handle your situation.

You have done this before. Find a time when you were at the effect of something and decided you had had enough. You had reached your limit and decided you were going to take some action. You then grabbed your situation by the horns and turned your problem around.

How did you feel the moment you took charge of your situation?

The moment you took charge of your situation you shifted from being at the effect to being at cause. Instantly you became alive again. You felt better about yourself and your life. You regained your power and your energy. The problem, which before was such a monster, was now just a small thing that needed to be handled.

You shifted your state of mind by generating a determination to handle your situation. You took charge of your life, and your life started working.

To the extent you live at cause, you will have a life that works. You will live in a state of confidence and effectiveness.

The key to living at cause is simple: don't stay at effect. As soon as you notice you are at effect, stop. Stop being at the effect of your situation and handle it. Handle your situation as fast as you can.

Sometimes you need to generate a lot of energy to create the determination necessary to handle a situation. This is especially true when you are deep at effect, but this is what you need to do if you want your life to work.

Take these steps to return to cause.

1. Notice that you are at the effect of something.

2. Remember that you have the ability to shift from being at the effect to being at cause.

3. List the specific circumstances you are at the effect of.

4. Generate a commitment and a determination to do whatever is necessary to handle each of your circumstances.

5. Take action.

The more you shift from effect to cause, the more you develop your ability to make the shift. You discover that living at effect is only a choice, a choice that produces needless suffering.

Practice making this shift as often as possible. Do this so you can master living at cause.

The next time you notice that you are at the effect, find the specific items you are at the effect of. List each one. Then generate the determination to handle your situation, and handle it as fast as you can.

The moment you take charge of your situation, you restore the experience of love. Your confidence and effectiveness return. Solutions appear and opportunities present themselves. Life seems to work for you rather than against you.

There is no situation that can't be handled once you generate the necessary commitment and determination. Situations usually get resolved so quickly you wonder why you waited so long to handle them.

You don't even need to know how to handle a particular situation. Once you have the commitment and determination, you will be able to find out.

Whenever you are at the effect of something, you suffer. When your life is full of items you are at the effect of, you suffer a lot.

What aspects of your life are you at the effect of? What aspects of your life don't work?

Notice how much you suffer by not handling these items. Notice how much these items drain you of your love, your aliveness and your peace of mind. Notice how these items rob you of your self-respect and your energy, and keep you from your dreams.

Each item in your life that you are at the effect of is an item that needs to be handled.

Imagine what your life would be like if you handled everything you are now at the effect of. What would life be like if everything flowed effortlessly and you were free to pursue your dreams? Take a moment and actually imagine this. Notice the freedom and self-respect you would have.

Now notice if you have any fear of having your life be totally effortless. Most people do. What is your fear? Be honest with yourself. Are you afraid you will blow the opportunity and have to face failure? Are you afraid to discover that you are responsible for every aspect of your life?

The fear of having life be effortless is very subtle yet can be very strong. To make sure we don't confront this fear, we stay at the effect and don't handle our lives.

To have your life be as miraculous as possible, discover your fears of having life be effortless. Then work with them until they are gone. If you have a fear of failing, be willing to fail. If you have a fear of discovering that you are responsible for your life, notice that you are responsible whether you like it or not.

Work with your fears; then ask yourself these questions: Are you willing to stop being at the effect of your life? Are you willing to take charge and handle every aspect of your life that doesn't work? Are you willing to have your life be effortless? Are you willing to set yourself free as an expression of love for yourself?

Living at effect seems safer and more comfortable than living at cause, but it isn't. Living at effect and not handling life produces pain and suffering. Living at cause and having life work produces love, aliveness and joy.

If you want a life of love, aliveness and joy, live your life at cause. Stop being at the effect of your life and handle it.

ACTION TO TAKE

◆ Notice what life is like when you are at the effect. Notice how discouraged you become and how much you suffer. Now recall a time when you shifted from effect to cause. Notice what your life was like after you made the shift.

◆ Are you willing to live your entire life at cause? Notice what a difference this would make in the quality of your life. Notice how effective you would be.

◆ Don't allow yourself to remain at the effect of anything. The moment you notice that you are at the effect of something, stop. Find what you are at the effect of and handle it. Live your life at cause.

◆ Practice making the shift from effect to cause. The more you make this shift, the more you master living at cause.

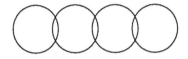

CHAPTER 8

CLEAN UP YOUR LIFE

The opportunity of life is to be free inside and to live in the experience of love. To the extent love and inner peace are present, life is effortless, full of aliveness and adventure.

Maintaining this experience of love can be very difficult when aspects of your life don't work.

The moment you are faced with an aspect of life that doesn't work, you get upset and close down. Aliveness and peace of mind disappear. You lose the experience of love.

If you want to be free inside and maintain the experience of love, you need to handle the items in your life that don't work. In other words, you need to clean up your life.

The first step in cleaning up your life is to discover the specific items that need to be handled. What are the items that pull you out of the experience of love? What aspects of your life do you get upset about?

Get a notebook and start listing every item in your life that you are at the effect of. List the big items and the small items. List the items that seem impossible. Even list the items you are not yet ready to handle. Write down everything in your life that bothers you.

Use the following categories or make up your own.

◆ Physical Environment

◆ Relationships

◆ Guilt and Wrongdoings

◆ Job and Career

◆ Finances

◆ Legal

◆ Health and Fitness

◆ Miscellaneous

Make sure every item of your life that doesn't work is listed somewhere. Be as specific as possible.

Physical Environment

Keep your physical environment clean and orderly. This includes your home, your car and your place of work.

Notice how you feel when you are in a car that is dirty and full of trash. Now notice how you feel when you are in a car that has just been washed and vacuumed. Notice the difference.

When your physical environment is sloppy and cluttered, your state of mind will be clouded and scattered. A clean and orderly environment supports a clear state of mind.

What aspects of your environment are you at the effect of? Is there a nail on the wall that always bothers you, but you never take the time to pull it out. Do you have a closet you hate to go into? Do you have a door that is always stuck? Is your car dented? Do you have a faucet that constantly drips. List every item in your physical environment that either needs to be cleaned up or in any way bothers you.

As you clean up your physical environment, you will notice an immediate difference inside. You will feel more alive and have more energy. You will feel better about yourself and your life.

Relationships

What relationships do you have that don't work? Who do you avoid or resent? Who can't you get along with? Who do you get upset about the moment you hear his or her name? List the name of each person that you are in any way upset about.

When you have relationships that don't work, you close down your love and keep your hurt from healing. You become protective and carry your upset to other relationships.

Relationships stop working when you stop accepting.

When you are resistant and critical toward someone, you tell the person that he or she isn't okay. The other person then gets upset and becomes resistant and critical toward you. Then you get more upset and critical toward the other. Then the other person does the same to you.

You create a cycle of conflict that goes on and on like a tennis volley without either person ever noticing his or her role in the conflict.

If you want to heal the hurt and have a relationship work, stop the volley of resistance and end the cycle of conflict.

Let go of your demands for how the person should be and accept the person the way he or she is. Forgive the person and be willing to feel your hurt. Then tell the person you want to heal your relationship. Acknowledge your role in the cycle of conflict and ask to be forgiven.

Restore the love in all your relationships.

Guilt and Wrongdoings

What have you done in the past that still weighs on you today? What do you feel guilty about? What are you hiding? What don't you want people to know about you? List every bad thing you have ever done from the time you were born until now. Be careful not to lie to yourself. If you have thoughts about something you have done, write it down.

After you complete your list, throw the list away. Acknowledging what you have done and putting it on paper will release much of your past. Now write the list of guilt and wrongdoings again. This second list will be much shorter and will show you the items you need to work on.

Past misdeeds are like heavy weights that slow you down. They inhibit your aliveness, your self-respect and your self-expression.

Do whatever is necessary to free yourself from the past. If you have guilt for something, forgive yourself. If you have done something bad to someone, go back to the person and clean up what you have done. Tell the person what you did and offer to make amends. If the person is impossible to find or is no longer alive, write the person an unaddressed letter or talk to the person in your imagination. If there is something you have done that you don't want anyone to know about, tell someone, tell several people.

The weight of your past deeds doesn't come from what you did. The weight comes from hiding, avoiding and withholding what you did. Once you are willing for anyone to know anything about you, you will have nothing to hide and you will be free. This doesn't mean call a press conference to expose your past, just be willing for anyone to know. The best way to do this is to tell some people. Keep in mind that everyone else has a similar list, and theirs is probably much worse than yours.

Being free of your past will be an enormous relief.

Job and Career

We spend most of our lives in some kind of job. You may be busy earning a living or taking care of a family. Your job, whatever it is, has an enormous impact on the quality of your life.

Does your job nurture you and fill you with love, aliveness and energy, or is your job a drain? Do you love your job or do you just endure? If you don't love what you do, you should consider doing something else. Life is too short to just endure. Find what you love to do, then find how to do it. You can discover a job and a career that you love if you really want to. If your job or career doesn't support you, put this on your list.

List anything about your job or career that bothers you. Do you have projects that are past due? Is your paperwork a mess? Are there certain conversations you need to have but have been avoiding? List anything concerning your job or your career that you are at the effect of.

Finances

If you are frequently upset about money, you have a condition that needs to be handled.

Money upsets seem to be due to a lack of income but this is seldom the case. Most money upsets are due to over-spending. When your expenses are more than your income, you can expect to be upset.

The key to true prosperity is to appreciate what you have and to spend less than you earn.

If your finances are a source of frequent upset, you may need to take some drastic action to handle your situation. You may need to change your lifestyle and reduce your expenses. You may need to move or sell some property. You may need to find another source of income? What action do you need to take?

If you have past due obligations, contact the people you owe and give them your plan for how and when the debt will be paid.

Making new financial arrangements can be a big relief. Make sure you keep any promises you make.

List everything you need to handle in the area of finance.

Legal

List everything of a legal nature that bothers you. Do you have a divorce or a lawsuit that weighs you down? Do you need a will? Do you have any unpaid traffic violations? Does your driver's license have your correct address? Do you owe back taxes? Is your insurance in order? List everything of a legal nature that you need to handle.

If you have a legal dispute, put your focus on finding solutions that work for everyone. When you put your focus on resolving the issues, the issues can get resolved and you can get on with your life.

When you put your focus on winning, you create a condition of adversariness that makes resolving issues very difficult.

By fighting to win, you force the other person to fight to avoid losing. You then have to fight to protect yourself from the other person. Then the other person has to fight even harder to be protected from you. You create a destructive cycle of conflict where coming out on top is all that matters.

When you don't focus on resolving the issues, the issues don't get resolved. The conflict can go on forever. If you want to end the conflict and get on with your life, stop being an adversary and find solutions where everyone can win.

Health and Fitness

What bothers you about your body or your health? Are you upset about your level of physical fitness or your appearance? Do you have physical ailments? Do you need a physical examination? Do your teeth need work? Do you need a new prescription for eye glasses? List everything about your body and your health that nags at you or concerns you.

Miscellaneous

List anything else that bothers you but doesn't fit under another category.

After you list everything in your life that you are at the effect of, the next step in cleaning up your life is to handle the items on your list.

To be most effective, find a buddy or some friends to work with. Make promises to each other about what you are going to handle and by when. A promise to a friend can give you the incentive to handle items you would otherwise put off. Group support is invaluable and can be a lot of fun.

The process of handling your life may take some time and some hard work, but the results will certainly be worth your effort.

Every time you handle an item, you will notice a difference inside. You will feel better about yourself and your life. You will have more energy and feel more alive.

If you only handle one item, won't your life be a little more enjoyable? What if you handle twenty per cent of what you are now at the effect of? Won't that make a big difference? What if you handle fifty per cent? What if you handle every item on your list?

Every step you take to clean up your life will make a difference.

You can have a life that works effortlessly if you want. You certainly have the ability. All you need is the commitment and determination to make it happen.

ACTION TO TAKE

◆ Get a notebook and make a list of everything you are at the effect of. List everything that pulls you out of the experience of love. List the big items, the small items and the items that seem impossible. Even list the items that you are not yet ready to handle.

◆ Handle the items on your list as fast as you can.

◆ Notice how you feel each time you handle something that has been bothering you. Notice how much energy and confidence you gain. Notice how free and alive you become.

◆ Find a buddy or some friends to work with. Make promises to each other about what you are going to handle and by when. Support each other and have fun in the process.

◆ Make cleaning up your life one of your highest priorities. Living in the experience of love is very difficult when life doesn't work.

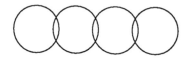

CHAPTER 9

BE FREE OF
GUILT AND RESENTMENT

Guilt and resentment are states of mind that destroy love. They seem to be caused by what happens but they're not. Guilt and resentment are caused by the way you react to what happens.

You create your own guilt and resentment. You can also release them. You can be free of all guilt and resentment if you want. Use this chapter to set yourself free of any guilt and resentment you have.

Guilt

Guilt robs you of your confidence and your self-respect. You feel undeserving and hold yourself back. Notice the price you pay for your guilt.

We create guilt to punish ourselves. We think that if we just punish ourselves enough, we will somehow make up for what we've done. We are our own judge and jury.

Maybe now you have suffered enough. Ask yourself, are you willing to be forgiven? Are you willing to be free of your guilt? Have you been punished enough?

If not, go get a big stick and beat yourself some more. Beat yourself until you feel sufficiently punished for whatever you have done. Then forgive yourself.

Select something you have done that you feel guilty about. Then use these questions to release your guilt:

◆ Did you do the thing for which you have guilt? Yes, you did. Face what you did and allow yourself to experience your hurt.

◆ At the moment you did whatever you did, didn't you see life in a very particular way?

◆ Don't you see life very differently now?

◆ When you did what you did, didn't you act

totally consistent with the way you were and the way you saw life at that particular moment?

◆ If you were wiser and more aware, if you knew then what you know today, couldn't you have acted very differently?

◆ Are you willing to forgive yourself for not having been wiser and more aware?

◆ Are you willing to forgive yourself for what you did, as a result of your limited awareness?

◆ Didn't you do the best you could with your limited awareness and ability?

◆ Do you now totally forgive yourself for not being wiser and more aware, and for doing whatever you did? Do you now let go of your guilt, just because you say so?

You did the best you could with the limited awareness you had. If you were wiser and more aware you could have acted very differently, but you weren't. You only knew what you knew at the time.

Even if you think you knew better, your degree of knowing wasn't sufficient to alter your actions. You didn't know back then what you know today.

"But I should have known." Nonsense. How could you possibly have known more than you did?

Five years from now you will be much wiser than you are today, but your future awareness is useless to you today. Likewise, your present awareness was useless to you back then. You only knew what you knew.

We go through life doing the best we can with limited equipment. We think we know but we don't. As a result we make mistakes. Sometimes we make big ones. That's how we learn.

The question is this, are you willing to forgive yourself for not knowing, for not being wiser and more aware? You might as well.

Forgive yourself for everything you have done from the time you were born until now. Work with each item of guilt until there are no more.

Resentments

When you have a resentment, a major part of you closes down. You become bitter and less able to express your love. You lose your aliveness and joy for life. You also make your life much more difficult.

When you resent someone you are saying, "I strongly dislike you." This instantly destroys the experience of love. The other person then gets upset and becomes resentful toward you. Then you resent the other person even more. Almost overnight, you create a cycle of conflict that produces tremendous suffering.

As long as you resent someone, a loving, supportive relationship with that person will be impossible.

We think that resentments are caused by the other person but they're not. No one has the power to create a resentment in you. Only you can do that.

That's why the same thing can happen to two different people and only one will have a resentment. Resentments are never a function of what happened. Resentments are a function of how you relate to what happened.

When you resent someone, you are saying very forcefully that the other person is the problem, the cause and the fault. Not you. You subconsciously keep the spotlight on the other person so you don't have to confront your hurt.

Resentments keep your hurt suppressed. Until you release your resentment, you will never heal your hurt.

If you want to end the cycle of conflict, re-store your love and heal your hurt, you need to release your resentments.

Ironically, you are the only one that really suffers when you resent. Notice the price you pay for your resentments. Notice how much resentments rob you of your aliveness and your peace of mind.

Releasing a resentment is not for the ben-efit of the other person. Releasing a resent-ment is for you. You release resentments so you can heal your hurt and become free inside.

The first step in releasing a resentment is to be willing to experience the hurt. Be willing to experience the loss of love and the feelings of being worthless or not good enough.

The next step is to make peace with what happened. Avoiding the hurt keeps you from being at peace. Once you are willing to expe-rience the hurt, you no longer need to resist what happened.

The last step is to stop blaming the person for what happened. Forgive. Forgive the person for the way he or she is and for what the person has done.

Forgiveness is a choice, a declaration, a form of letting go. "I am angry and hurt, but I forgive. I forgive just because I say so."

You can forgive and still be upset. Anger and hurt are separate from resentment. Resentment is the avoidance of these feelings. Once you forgive, you release the avoidance and the anger and hurt soon disappear.

Once you become free of your resentment, you physically feel the return of your aliveness. You restore the experience of love and your peace of mind. You become free of your upset and able to interact with the other person in a way that works.

To release a resentment, you must first be willing to let it go. Are you willing to be free of your resentments?

Select a resentment you want to release.

Then use the following questions to release your resentment and make peace with what happened. Work with each question until you can say "yes," and mean it.

If you notice resistance to saying "yes," look for the hurt you are avoiding. Allow yourself to experience any hurt that gets reactivated. Keep in mind that the purpose of releasing a resentment is to set yourself free.

♦ Are you willing to be free of your resentment?

♦ Are you willing to feel all the hurt from what happened, and the feelings of being worthless and not good enough?

♦ Is the person you resent the way he or she is?

♦ Is the person that way whether you like it or not?

♦ Are you willing for the person to be the way he or she is?

♦ Are you willing to forgive the person for being that way?

♦ Doesn't the person have a very particular view of life?

♦ Is the person going to have that view of

life whether you are willing or not?

♦ Are you willing to let the person have his or her own way of viewing life?

♦ Does that person act consistent with his or her view of life?

♦ If the person saw life differently, and was wiser and more aware, couldn't the person have acted very differently?

♦ Are you willing to forgive the person for not being wiser and more aware? Notice that the person doesn't have much choice about his or her level of awareness.

♦ Are you willing to forgive the person for acting consistent with his or her limited view of life? Again, notice that the person doesn't have much choice.

♦ Are you willing to forgive the person for doing what he or she did, as a result of this limited awareness?

♦ Do you now forgive the person for being the way he or she is, for having a limited awareness, and for doing what he or she did?

♦ Do you now let go of all resentment for the

person, just because you say so?

If you say "no" to any of these questions, that's where you're stuck. Keep working with each question until you can say "yes."

If you have any resentment left, see if you can release it by your declaration. "I now release all resentment for that person, just because I say so."

You can release a resentment in an instant. That's how long it took for you to put it there. Sometimes releasing a resentment takes longer. Sometimes you have to forgive over and over again until the resentment is gone.

If you have trouble letting go of a resentment, look for what you are avoiding. What would you have to experience or be responsible for if you lost your resentment? Find what you are avoiding and be willing to experience it.

Each time you release a resentment you will feel a freedom inside. Aliveness and peace of mind return. You restore your compassion and your ability to love.

List all your resentments and do whatever it takes to release each one. The quality of your life depends on it.

ACTION TO TAKE

◆ List everything you have ever done that you feel guilty about.

◆ List the name of every person you resent.

◆ Does your guilt and resentment change anything? Notice how much guilt and resentment damages your love, your aliveness and your peace of mind.

◆ Are you willing to be free of all guilt and resentment? If not, what are you avoiding?

◆ Use the questions in this chapter to be free of all your guilt and resentment. Work with the questions until you are totally free of all guilt and resentment.

◆ Make sure you don't create any new guilt or resentment. Learn to forgive yourself and others.

CHAPTER 10

HEAL YOUR RELATIONSHIPS

We all want to be loved, accepted and appreciated, just the way we are. When we feel loved and appreciated by someone, we come alive. We feel better about ourselves and the people around us. We feel happy and free. Everything seems to work. Life flows.

This is the love we want so much in our relationships. When this love is present, relationships are nurturing and supportive. When this love is absent, relationships are painful and destructive.

The presence or absence of this love seems to be a function of other people, but it isn't. The presence or absence of love is a function of how you interact with other people.

Every time you interact with another person you either create love or destroy love, and whatever you give comes right back.

You create love by giving acceptance and appreciation. When you give acceptance and appreciation the other person feels better about him or herself and naturally becomes more accepting and appreciative toward you.

You destroy love by being non-accepting and critical. As you give non-acceptance, the other person gets upset and automatically becomes critical toward you. Then you get upset and become more critical toward the other. Then the other person becomes more critical toward you.

You create a cycle of conflict that destroys relationships and produces tremendous suffering.

If you have any relationship that isn't working, this cycle of conflict is present. To heal the relationship and restore the love, you need to end the cycle.

You can do this with only one person. The cycle of conflict is like a tennis volley. Two people are needed to keep the cycle going.

All you need to end the cycle is for one person to refuse to play the game.

You stop playing the game when you give acceptance and appreciation instead of being critical and resentful.

To make the shift from criticalness to acceptance, you need to heal the issues in you that create your resistance and keep you from accepting.

Use the following steps to heal these issues and to restore love in each of your relationships. Work with one relationship at a time.

1. Give the other person full permission to be the way he or she is.

Notice that the person you resist has a particular way of behaving and a particular view of life. Notice that the person is this way whether you like it or not. Accepting is nothing more than surrendering to the truth.

Let go of your demands and expectations for how the person should be and make peace with the way the person is. Stop trying to change the person.

If the person isn't for you, you don't have to

spend time with the person or live with the person. You can let the person be the way he or she is — somewhere else. If leaving is not an alternative, you better make peace with the way the person is.

List the characteristics you can't stand in the person and give each characteristic permission to be there.

Say these words, "I give you full permission to be the way you are and to never change. I give up my right to complain about the way you are." Say these words and mean it.

2. Let the person go.

If you are currently in a relationship, make sure you are willing for the person to be gone tomorrow.

Do every thing you can to create an environment where the person will never want to leave, but in your heart, be willing for the person to go.

When you hang on to someone, you suffocate the person and force the person to withdraw. When the person pulls back, you get upset. You destroy the experience of love and push the person even further away.

You create the cycle of conflict and put your relationship in danger. You become so full of fear and upset that you can't see what needs to be done. All you can do is resist.

When the person finally leaves, the fear of losing someone turns into anger and resentment. Then you move on, find someone else and repeat the whole process.

The fear of losing someone is one of the biggest destroyers of relationships.

Take a look at your life. Are you willing to be alone? Are you willing to lose your relationship? Are you willing for the person to be happy without you? If you have trouble with any of these questions, look for what you are really avoiding. What would you have to experience if you lost whoever you are hanging on to?

Are you willing to experience the hurt from the past? Are you willing to let go of your dreams for how it could have been? Are you willing to face your fear of not being able to make it on your own? Are you willing to experience the hurt of not being good enough or not being worth loving?

Find what you are avoiding and then be willing to experience it. Be willing to experience the hurt, the loss and the feelings of not being worth loving. Once you are willing to experience this hurt, you no longer need to hang on. You can let the person go.

Say these words either to yourself or to the other person, "I give you full permission to leave, to be gone from my life forever. I want you to stay, but I want you to be happy. If you have to go, you have my blessings." Say this and be willing to experience all the hurt that gets reactivated. Say this and mean it.

Let the person go and put your focus on restoring the love in your relationship, one human being to another.

Once you are willing to lose someone, you stop being run by fear and become able to see what needs to be done.

You also treat the person very differently. When you know that someone can be gone tomorrow, you will treasure every moment you have with the person today. You become very accepting and appreciative.

3. Accept full responsibility for what happened.

When you blame someone, you destroy love.

You resist the person and create resistance against yourself.

A very effective way to stop the blaming, heal your relationship and restore your peace of mind, is to discover your responsibility for what happened.

Your responsibility is there. The only question is whether you are willing to see it. If you doubt that you are responsible, just ask the other person.

Usually we only notice how the other person treats us. Then we react accordingly. We don't notice that we have anything to do with what happens.

Actually, you have everything to do with what happens. The other person is constantly reacting to you. How you treat the other person determines what that reaction will be.

If someone has an affair, that person is clearly responsible. So is the spouse. People usually have affairs to find love and appreciation. If this was sufficiently provided by the spouse, there wouldn't have been an affair. Both people are fully responsible.

Once you discover your responsibility for what happened, you can no longer blame the other person. You also make it much more difficult for the other person to resist you.

When you point your finger at someone, you naturally create resistance. When you stop blaming and point at yourself, this resistance disappears.

Take a moment now and find your responsibility for what happened.

Notice how you single-handedly destroyed the love in your relationship. Notice how non-accepting, judgmental and critical you were. You didn't make sure the other person felt loved, accepted and appreciated. You pushed the person away.

Notice how the other person's actions have just been a reaction to you. Notice how you forced the other person to protect him or herself from you. Notice how you created and maintained the cycle of conflict.

The other person is also fully responsible, but so what? Blaming doesn't change a thing and almost always makes your situation worse.

By accepting full responsibility for what happened, you regain your power. You stop being at the effect of the other person and become able to interact in a way that heals your relationship and handles your situation.

4. Forgive the person.

Nothing destroys the experience of love faster and more powerfully than a resentment. Resentments are the exact opposite of accepting and appreciating someone.

When you resent someone, you forcefully communicate your non-acceptance. The other person then gets hurt, becomes upset and then gives it right back to you. Resentments create very destructive relationships.

The key to releasing a resentment is to be willing to experience the hurt. Then forgive the person for being the way he or she is and for not being wiser and more aware. Forgive the person for acting consistent with his or her limited awareness.

Remember that forgiveness is a choice and is not for the benefit of the other person. The purpose of forgiving is to heal your hurt and to set yourself free.

Use the questions in the previous chapter to release your resentments.

5. See that you are just like the other person.

Any characteristic you resist in another person is actually an aspect of you that you are not at peace with. You may not act exactly like the other person, but the characteristic is still in you.

As long as you resist this aspect of you, you will resist the other person. The moment you see that you are just like the other person, your resistance turns into compassion and your relationship heals.

If you don't believe that the characteristics you resist are in you, notice how you would feel if someone said you were exactly like the person you resist. You wouldn't like it. You would resist even the thought. You would resist because the thought strikes a nerve.

You create the nerve by resisting this aspect of you and by resisting all the hurt associated with feeling this way in the past.

Until you heal this nerve and become at peace with this aspect of you, you will automatically resist anyone that demonstrates the same characteristic. No one having this characteristic will ever have a chance with you. Your relationships will be doomed before they even start.

The problem always seems to be the other person but the problem is actually you. You can't be at peace with the characteristic.

Resisting this characteristic also brings more people with this characteristic into your life, and the more you resist the characteristic, the more this kind of person will show up.

List the characteristics you can't stand in the person you resist. Then work with each characteristic until you can recognize and make peace with that same characteristic in you. If this is difficult, review the chapter on loving yourself.

Once you can see that you are just like the other person, your resistance turns into compassion and your relationship heals. Until you see that you are just like the other person, your resistance will continue.

6. Get with the person and clean up your relationship.

Once you are at peace with the other person, you can interact in a way that communicates acceptance and appreciation.

Your next step is to meet with the person

and take responsibility for what happened. Do this in person if you can. If you can't, do it by telephone or by letter.

This is the fastest way to end the cycle of conflict. It clears the past and lets the other person know you are playing a different game now.

Tell the other person that you are responsible for what happened and that you want your relationship to work. Tell how you destroyed the love and created the cycle of conflict. Apologize for all the hurt and suffering you caused. Ask the person to forgive you.

By asking for forgiveness, you express humility and create an opportunity for the other person to make peace with you. Even if the person refuses, forgiveness is usually just a matter of time.

Encourage the person to say whatever he or she is upset about. Upsets only do damage when they are kept inside. Once upsets are communicated they lose their power and disappear.

Listen to whatever the person has to say. Don't fight or resist anything. Even if the person's communication is untrue, it's true to the other person and that's what counts. If you feel hurt, let the other person know, but don't blame or try to change the person.

Make sure the person feels loved, accepted and appreciated. To do this, you may have to set aside your ego. but this is a small price to pay for freedom.

Remember, you don't have to live with the person or spend time together, just restore the love, one human being to another.

As you restore the love, you heal both your relationship and your hurt. You set yourself free of the conflict and suffering. You become more alive and more able to express your love.

To the extent your relationships are an expression of love, you will have a life that is nurturing and supportive.

Take your list of painful relationships and do whatever it takes to heal each one.

To be more effective in relationships, read my other book, *How To Heal A Painful Relationship.*

ACTION TO TAKE

◆ List the name of every person that you resist. Who don't you get along with? Who do you avoid or resent? List the name of every person with whom you are upset.

◆ Notice how much you suffer when your relationships don't work. Notice what happens to your aliveness and your peace of mind.

◆ Are you willing to clean up your relationships and restore the experience of love in you? If not, what are you avoiding?

◆ If you are ready to heal your relationships, use the steps outlined in this chapter. Work with your relationships until each one becomes an expression of love.

◆ Make sure you don't create any new painful relationships. Make sure the people in your life feel loved, accepted and appreciated. Give up your rules for how people should be and see the love and beauty in everyone, just the way they are.

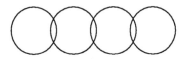

CHAPTER 11

BE PROSPEROUS

Most of us sabotage our own prosperity. We limit our financial growth and set up ourselves for frequent upset.

We think that the problem is the lack of income, but this is seldom the case. Most of the people in this world would love to have your level of income. The problem is how we handle the income that we have.

We overspend. We use every resource available to raise our standard of living, and when credit is available, we use that too. The result is a lifestyle where expenses equal or exceed the income.

When this happens, you can expect to be

upset. No matter what your income is, it will soon be gone. You will never have enough. You will constantly experience fear and insufficiency.

If you could somehow set up your affairs so that your expenses were ten per cent less than your income, you would have a very different life. You would be free of financial upset and would soon experience prosperity.

Imagine what your level of prosperity would be like if you took ten per cent of everything you earned from the time you were eighteen and invested it wisely. You would feel very prosperous.

But this isn't the way we handle our affairs. We overspend. We overspend so we can get more of what we want. We are driven by our wants. No matter what we have, we still want more. Our wants are insatiable.

If you made a list of everything you wanted, and received everything on your list, before long, you would have a new list of wants.

You can never get enough of what you want because the void you are trying to fill is inside yourself, not outside.

Until you heal this inner void, you will continue to sabotage your prosperity. Instead of building an estate, you will overspend. Instead of creating a life of abundance, you will create a life of fear, upset and insufficiency.

To heal this inner void, find the core issue that drives your insatiable wants.

The first step in finding your issue is to notice the feelings you have when you first overspend. How do you feel about yourself when you get the things that you want? How would you feel about yourself if you received everything on your list of wants? What kind of person would you be? Would you be successful, important or worthy? Take a moment and look.

Now look at the opposite. How would you feel about yourself if you lost everything. What would you have to experience about yourself if you lost your job, your home and all your possessions? Actually imagine this happening. What aspect of you would you have to face if you had nothing? Would you have to face being a failure, a loser, unimportant or worthless?

Find the characteristic you would have to face. Avoiding this characteristic creates the issue that drives your insatiable wants. To avoid the feeling of being a failure, for example, you will need to get as much as you can so you will feel like a success.

Unfortunately, the feelings of success are very temporary. When you have trouble paying your bills you will feel even more like a failure.

To heal your issue, you need to make peace with this aspect of you. Allow yourself to experience the feelings of being a failure or whatever your issue is. Allow yourself to experience the hurt.

Then be willing to have nothing.

When you can have nothing and still be happy, you will be free. You will have control over your wants. You will be free of fear and upset over money. You will be more creative, more effective and more able to have what you want.

Are you willing to have nothing? Are you willing to be homeless? What would you have to experience if you lost everything? What aspect of you would you have to face? Find the experience you are avoiding and be willing to experience it. Continue to work with this until you can have nothing and still be happy.

Once you are truly willing to have nothing, you will deeply appreciate whatever you have. You can then experience true prosperity.

True prosperity is appreciating what you have, being free inside and going for your dreams.

If wealth is one of your dreams, go for your dream with all of your heart. Just make sure you have fun in the process. Make sure the process of becoming wealthy is a game rather than a matter of survival. Keep your focus on being free inside.

To be free inside, you may need to lower your expenses. Lower your expenses so you can invest at least ten per cent of everything you earn. This financial cushion will help free you of upset and at the same time, allow you to build an estate.

What do you need to do to make sure your expenses are at least ten per cent less than your income? Do you need to move or sell some property? Do you need to restructure your debt? Create a plan for what you need to do and then make it happen. The process of reducing expenses may take time, but the end result will certainly be worth your effort.

Live a simple life that works. Spend less

---

than you earn. Be free of financial upset and go for your dreams.

ACTION TO TAKE

◆ Notice the damage overspending has caused in your life. Notice the fear, the upsets and the feelings of insufficiency that come from overspending.

◆ Find the core issue that fuels your insatiable wants and forces your overspending. Find what you would have to experience about yourself if you had nothing. Make peace with that aspect of you.

◆ Be willing to have nothing and appreciate what you have. Work with this until you can live in poverty and still be happy. Then notice the abundance you have in your life. Be very thankful for all that you have.

◆ Set up your financial affairs so that you spend at least ten per cent less than you earn. Take the remaining ten per cent and invest it wisely. Create a plan for how you will accomplish this.

◆ Lead a simple life that works. Don't overspend.

PART III

◆

CONNECT WITH YOUR LIFE FORCE

As you open your heart and clean up your life, you set yourself free. You become an expression of love and aliveness.

This love and aliveness is your life force, the very essence of who you are. To the extent you bring this forth, you create a life that will exceed your dreams.

Your next step is to find an expression for your love. Learn to express the essence of you in a way that creates joy, fulfills your purpose and allows you to become one with your life force.

CHAPTER 12

RELEASE YOUR UPSETS

The natural state of who you are is love. When you experience this state, you feel free and alive. You have a deep inner peace and are full of joy. This state is the very essence of who you are.

When you get upset, this state disappears. You lose your aliveness and your ability to see what needs to be done. You lose your natural effectiveness.

To restore the state of love and inner peace, you need to release your upsets.

Upsets seem to be caused by circumstances but they're not. Upsets are caused by how you relate to circumstances. Upsets are caused by you. You create your own upsets. You can also release them.

Learning to release your upsets is one of the most important tools for having a life of love and inner peace.

To release an upset, there are a number of steps you can take.

1. Notice you are having an upset.

Circumstances don't make you upset, you do. Whenever you are upset, there is something you are resisting. Once you realize that you are creating your own upset, you have the power to set yourself free.

2. Be willing to be free of your upset.

Do you want to be free inside or do you want to be upset? If you want to be upset, ask yourself why. What do you gain by staying upset? Work with this until you are willing to be free of your upset.

3. Find the specific circumstances you are resisting.

Go back to the moment the upset began and state what happened. Don't add any judgment or emotion, just state the facts. What happened? What thoughts did you have? What are the circumstances you don't like? What are you afraid to lose? What do you fear will happen? Be as specific as possible.

4. Notice that the circumstances are in your life whether you like it or not.

Notice how irrelevant your wants and feelings are. Your circumstances are in your life no matter how upset you become. Being upset doesn't change a thing except inside you.

5. Separate yourself from the circumstances.

Notice that the circumstances and your feelings are two separate things. The circumstances aren't causing your upset. Your upset comes from past hurt. Take your focus off the circumstances and put your focus on the hurt.

6. Find the feelings and emotions you are avoiding.

What feelings and emotions are reactivated by your circumstances? What would you have to experience if your circumstances stayed forever? What would you have to experience if your fears were to happen or if you lost whatever you are hanging on to? What is the hurt you are avoiding? What do you have to face about yourself?

7. Be willing to experience all the feelings and emotions that are being reactivated.

Let the hurt come and let it go. You are experiencing this hurt anyway, so you might as well give your hurt permission to be there. Be like a young child. Cry if you can. Allow yourself to feel the hurt and the feelings of being not okay. Remind yourself that you will be fine. Once you are willing to feel the hurt, you no longer need to resist the circumstances.

8. Give your circumstances full permission to be in your life.

You don't have to like your circumstances, just give them permission to be in your life.

Tell your circumstances, "You can be in my life as long as you want." Tell your fear, "I give you full permission to happen." Give your permission over and over again until you can say it and mean it. Be willing to experience all the emotion that gets reactivated.

Giving permission is nothing more than surrendering to the truth. Your circumstances are in your life whether you give them permission to be there or not. Let go of your demands for how you say life should be and make peace with the way your life is.

9. Notice the freedom and peace that comes from letting go.

The moment you stop resisting, you release your upset and set yourself free inside. You see your situation very differently. You see solutions you couldn't see before. You restore your peace of mind and your joy for life.

10. Take whatever action you need to take.

Set yourself free inside. Then do whatever you need to do. Action that is free of upset will be naturally effective and supportive.

Use your upsets to discover the hurt that needs to be healed.

Whenever you get upset, your circumstances have just struck a nerve. This nerve is hurt from the past and feelings of not being okay or good enough. Until you heal this hurt, you will continue to get upset and make your life more difficult.

What nerves do you have? What do you get upset about? Find your nerves and work to heal them.

Use the steps in this chapter to release your upsets. Every time you release an upset, you see more of the truth and heal more of your hurt.

Once you heal the hurt, the same circumstances can happen again, and you won't get hooked. You remain free of upset, able to see what needs to be done.

As you learn to release your upsets, you soon discover that upsets are just a choice. You never have to be upset. You can live your life in a state of love, freedom and inner peace.

Release your upsets as fast as you can. Get used to living in the experience of love.

ACTION TO TAKE

◆ Notice what happens to the experience of love when you get upset. Notice how much you suffer and notice what happens to your effectiveness.

◆ What would life be like if you were free of upset? Actually imagine this. Notice how much happier and more effective you would be. Are you willing to give up being upset?

◆ Make a list of everything you get upset about. For each upset, look for the nerve that gets struck.

◆ Start the process of healing these nerves. Some nerves heal quickly; others take time. Work with each upset until you heal the hurt. When the hurt is healed, the same circumstances can happen again, and you won't get upset.

◆ Practice releasing your upsets. Whenever you get upset, use the steps in this chapter to set yourself free. Get used to living in the experience of love, free of fear and upset.

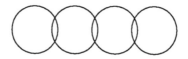

CHAPTER 13

GO FOR YOUR DREAMS

When you go for your dreams, life becomes an adventure. You have a direction, a reason for living. You add spice to your life.

What are your dreams? What are you going for in your life?

If you don't have a dream to go for, get one as fast as you can. When you don't have a dream, life stops being an adventure and becomes something you have to endure.

To discover your dreams, get some paper and list everything you love and appreciate. "I love going for a walk early in the morning. I love the sea. I love to travel and to see people in love. I love my friends and I love flowers."

List everything you can think of. Let your thoughts flow. What do you love? What do you enjoy? Write pages and pages if you can. The more you write, the more you will get excited about life and the more you will discover your dreams.

After you list everything you love, start listing your dreams. What do you want to have? What do you want to do? What do you want to accomplish? What are your dreams? Don't limit yourself by what you think is possible. Allow yourself to dream big dreams.

All your dreams can come true, even the big ones. If you have the ability to dream about something, you have the ability to have the dream come true.

Often we believe something is impossible, so we never allow ourselves to have the dream. The dream could come true, we just don't let it happen.

In one of our workshops, we do an exercise that demonstrates this. You can do the same exercise.

Make a list of everything that you believe is required in order to be wealthy. Do you have to have a good education? Do you have to come from a wealthy family? Do you have to be a workaholic? What is required in order to be wealthy? Take a few minutes and list each requirement.

After you complete your list, take each requirement and notice if there are any exceptions. If there is an exception to any item on your list, then the item isn't really a requirement.

Review your list of requirements and notice that there are exceptions to every one. People have become wealthy with no education, from poor backgrounds and without being a workaholic. There will be an exception to every requirement you can think of.

Nothing is required for a dream to come true unless you say so. If you believe a dream is impossible, that becomes the truth, but only for you.

To have a dream come true, there may be some steps to take and obstacles to overcome, but your dream can come true.

One of the most powerful steps for having a dream come true is to know that the dream is on the way. You can create this knowing by doing the following exercise.

Select the dream you want to have come

true. Do you want to have a new relationship or a new job? Do you want to handle a specific area of your life?

Select your dream. Then close your eyes and imagine that your dream has already happened. Make the dream a reality in your imagination. Experience your dream in great detail.

If your dream is a new relationship, imagine having a romantic, candlelight dinner with a very special person. Hold each other's hand while walking on a secluded beach. Experience being madly in love with each other. Make the dream real.

While you are making your dream real, keep your eyes closed and add feelings of intense joy and thankfulness. Hurray! Hurray! How wonderful this is! Create such an experience of joy and thankfulness that you are grinning from ear to ear. The intense feelings of joy and thankfulness are necessary to erase the limitations and restrictions that keep your dream at a distance.

After you have done this for a minute, release your dream to God. Then bask in the joy and happiness, knowing that your dream is on the way.

Once you know that your dream is on the

way, your situation will seem very different. You will see possibility and opportunity you could never have seen before.

Now you may need to take some action. What action do you need to take for your dream to come true? What is the next step?

You won't know all the steps to your dream, but if you listen to your intuition, you will know the next step, and then the next step. Each time you take a step, you discover a little more of the path and get a little closer to your dream.

Sometimes you may trip and fall down. When this happens, pick yourself up and then take the next step. If you keep taking the next step and never give up, you will eventually get to your dream.

Go for your dream at full speed, but don't get too serious. Remember that life is just a game. Going for your dreams is much more important than having your dreams come true.

Besides, the more you need your dreams, the more your dreams will elude you. When obstacles appear, you will become full of fear and upset. You will lose your creativity and the ability to see what needs to be done.

Be willing for your dreams to never happen, and at the same time, do everything you can to make your dreams come true.

Go for your dreams like you are playing a game. When you do this, your life becomes an exciting adventure.

ACTION TO TAKE

◆ Go for your dreams with all your heart. Life becomes an adventure when you have something to go for.

◆ If you don't have any dreams to go for, find some.

◆ Get a notebook and write down everything you love. Let your thoughts flow and write everything down. Write pages and pages if you can. Then write down your dreams. Write down everything you would like to have or do. Get excited about your dreams.

◆ Know that your dreams will come true. Create this knowing by doing the visualization exercise. Do this with each of your dreams.

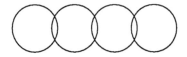

CHAPTER 14

FIND YOUR LIFE PURPOSE

Everyone has a particular life expression, or purpose. When you live your purpose, you feel fulfilled. You love what you do and know you make a difference. Your life has meaning and direction.

Purpose is the natural expression of who you are. Purpose utilizes all your gifts, your talents and your abilities. You are good at your purpose and love what you do.

Until you find your purpose, there will always seem to be something missing in life.

Unfortunately, finding your purpose is much easier said than done. You can't go to the library and look up your purpose. You won't find purpose in the want ads. Purpose is something you create. Purpose is something you bring forth out of your commitment.

Although you can't look up purpose, there is a path where purpose can be discovered.

The first step on this path is to find your passion. What do you love to do? What are you naturally good at? What turns you on? What could you throw your heart and soul into? What do you love doing so much, that you would pay for the privilege of doing it?

The process of discovering your passion can take months of active looking, so be patient.

After you find your passion, the next step is to find a way to live your passion full time, and still pay the bills.

This may seem impossible but it's not. There is a way to do what you love. Your job is to discover how.

Constantly ask yourself the question, "How can I earn a living doing what I love?" Explore every possibility and turn over every stone. Keep searching for a way.

Pray for guidance and follow your intuition. Maybe you need to get a different job or go back to school. Trust yourself, and keep taking the next step.

The process may take years, but once you have the commitment to discover and live your passion, you will eventually find a way.

Passion usually doesn't pay much at first, so lower your expenses as much as possible. When you need a large monthly income, you eliminate most of your opportunities.

Once you find a way to earn a living doing what you love, your life will never be the same. You get to spend the rest of your life having fun instead of working. You also become very effective at what you do, and eventually, if you want, you can provide a good income for yourself.

While you are looking for your passion, find the contribution you want to make to the world. Do you want to teach people how to love? Do you want to clean up the environment or show people how to have fun? What is the contribution you want to make?

When you can do what you love, and at the same time make a difference in people's lives, your passion gains a power that can move mountains.

When your passion and your contribution become one, you have found your purpose.

The following questions can give you some good insight into your purpose. Write down every thought you have in response to a question. Keep writing until there is no more response. Look for your passion and your contribution.

◆ What are your dreams?

◆ What do you love to do? What makes you come alive?

◆ What are you good at? What are your gifts, your talents and your abilities?

◆ What were you doing when you were the happiest?

◆ What aspects or characteristics of you are you proud of?

◆ What have you done that you are proud of?

◆ How would you like the world to be?

◆ When you were young, what did you know you would do when you grew up?

◆ When you are on your deathbed, what would you regret not having done?

◆ If you could do absolutely anything in your life, without any restriction, what would you do?

◆ If you could make any contribution to the world, what would it be?

◆ What is your passion?

◆ What is your contribution?

◆ What is your purpose?

Keep looking for your passion and the contribution you want to make.

The next level of purpose is giving your life to serving others and to serving God. This isn't for everyone, but for those who are called, this step is by far the most rewarding.

To be most effective in your serving, find the specific result you want to produce through your contribution. Have the result be more than you can ever accomplish, then dedicate your life to producing that result.

For example, you may want to give your life to ending hunger or cleaning up the environment. You may want to find homes for the homeless or you may want to teach the world to love.

Mother Teresa gave her life to serving the poorest of the poor. Martin Luther King dedicated his life to gaining equal rights for everyone.

Say this prayer, "God, I give you my life, my heart and my soul. How can I serve you? What do you want me to do? My life is yours." Ask for direction and follow your guidance.

Find the specific result you want to produce, then do everything you can to make it happen. Keep asking yourself the question, "What needs to be done to produce the result?"

By giving your life to something bigger and more important than you, you set aside much of your ego. You take the focus off of yourself and allow your love and your greatness to come forth.

Albert Schweitzer once said, "Those among you who will be truly happy are those who have sought and have found how to serve."

By doing what you love and finding how to serve, you add a very special joy to life.

ACTION TO TAKE

◆ Start the process of discovering and then living your life purpose. The process begins the moment you start looking. Your commitment will show you the way.

◆ Use the questions in this chapter to gain insight into your purpose. Write down every thought you have in response to a question. Keep writing until there is no more response. Use the questions to bring forth desires that are deep inside.

◆ The process of discovering and then living your purpose can take years. Be patient and at the same time, don't ever stop. Follow your intuition and keep taking the next step.

◆ Find your way to serve and start serving. Have your life be about something bigger and more important than you.

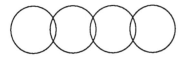

CHAPTER 15

EXPERIENCE YOUR SPIRITUALITY

There is a special light in each of us. This light is the love that you are.

This love is also your life force. As you allow your love to come forth, you experience the essence of life. You are happy and alive. Life is a joy.

When your love is suppressed, you disconnect from your life force. You lose your joy and create a life of darkness, a life of fear and upset.

The opportunity of life is to connect with your life force. You make this connection through your spirituality.

There is a higher power that is the source and the essence of love. To me, this power is God. As you connect with God and experience the presence of God in your life, you enter the garden of Eden.

You also tap into a power much greater than you. You become the hands and feet of God. You become a channel for God's love, and the universe moves to support you.

You make the connection with God by bringing forth your love. To bring forth your love, do the following:

♦ **Open your heart.** Let go of your walls and be willing to be hurt. Allow yourself to be like a young child.

♦ **Love yourself.** Stop trying to be what you are not, and see the beauty in the way that you are. Love and accept every aspect of yourself.

♦ **Trust.** Trust that you will be okay no matter what happens. Trust, just because you say so.

♦ **Let go.** Let go of your demands for how life should be and make peace with the way your life is. Set yourself free inside.

Then do whatever you need to do. Stop resisting.

◆ **Clean up your life.** Handle the aspects of life that pull you out of the experience of love. Live at cause.

◆ **Release your upsets.** Restore the experience of love as fast as you can. Don't stay upset. Forgive.

◆ **Express your love.** See the beauty in every person and every aspect of life.

As you bring forth your love, you remove the blocks that keep you separate from God. As you remove these blocks, you experience the presence of God in your life.

Another important part of the connection is your relationship with God. A personal relationship will allow you to be in communication and to receive special guidance.

To create a personal relationship, all you have to do is want one, and the more you want the relationship, the faster the relationship will come.

For years I had a prayer. "Take me, God, I'm yours. Take me, God, I'm yours." I would say this over and over, always adding at the end, "if you are there." I didn't know if there was a God, but if there was, I wanted God to take me. Eventually, my prayers were answered.

Give your life to God and ask for a relationship. Your prayers will be answered and your relationship will come.

You hear God most clearly when you are still and at peace inside. When your mind is racing, you can't hear the voice from within.

There are several ways to still the mind. One way is to let go. When you are resisting, your mind goes ninety miles an hour. When you stop resisting, your mind becomes still.

Another way to still the mind is to meditate. Get in a comfortable position and close your eyes. Create the feeling of intense joy, then bask in the love and peace of God. Allow your thoughts to have their say and then be still. Move toward the silence.

In the silence you can communicate. Speak to God and listen for the response. Listen for your guidance.

Each person has a different way of experiencing the presence of God. Some people experience God by being in nature. Some experience God by going to a particular church service. Others make the connection by praying and meditating. Find the way that works best for you.

I make my connection by going to a small Catholic mass during the week. During the mass, I go into a meditative state and experience being in the presence of God. This restores my love and inner peace.

Making this connection is like recharging the batteries to your life force. The more you make the connection, the more your life works. Make the connection every day.

One day my brother was making the connection and had an experience that permanently altered his life. While he was praying he felt something take his hand and lead him to his desk. He then started to write a letter, but he wasn't the author.

Here is the letter.

Dear Randy,
Trust me. I will guide you. You don't know and I do. I love you more than you know. I am the source of all you desire. You can only succeed by surrendering to my will. You think you know the way but you don't. Learn to listen to me. Only I am the source of joy

and fulfillment. You will never truly get what you want on your own. I am what your heart yearns for. Serve me.

                                             God

The letter speaks a profound truth. We think we know the way, but we don't. Believing that we know keeps us stuck forever. By giving your life to God and listening to God's guidance, you can be lead to a life of joy and fulfillment.

Give your life to God and allow yourself to be managed. Listen to your guidance and do what you are told.

One of the best ways to receive guidance is to trust your intuition. Listen to your heart.

There is a very big difference between listening to your head and listening to your heart. When you listen to your head, you listen to your computer. You hear all your decisions from the past. When you follow your head, you are guaranteed to extend your past into the future.

When you listen to your heart, you receive guidance from an unlimited reality, a power much wiser than you. You receive the guidance that will lead you out of your past and take you where you need to go.

Your heart will always guide you in the direction of love. Learn to listen to your heart and do what your heart says. Follow your heart even when the guidance doesn't seem to make sense. The more you follow your heart, the louder your heart will speak.

If you are willing, you can be led to a life that will exceed your dreams. Every aspect of your life can be effortless, an expression of love and joy. Every relationship can be loving and supportive. Finances can be handled forever. You can be vital and alive. You can know you make a difference.

Your life can become the exciting adventure it once was. You can be free and alive like a young child. You can do what you love. You can experience the thrill of going for your dreams, and you can watch your dreams come true.

You can also experience a confidence and an inner peace you never dreamed possible. You can be fulfilled and have a life of meaning and purpose.

All of this is possible when you let go of your life and put your focus on restoring love and connecting with your life force.

ACTION TO TAKE

♦ Make the connection with your life force. Create a personal relationship with God, so you can receive guidance and have your life be more fulfilling.

♦ Make this your prayer, "God, I give you my life, my heart and my soul. I give you my relationships, my property and my health. What do you want me to do? How can I serve you?"

♦ Listen to your heart and follow your guidance.

♦ Trust that you will always be taken care of. Know that whatever happens in your life is for your highest good. Let go, and know that you will be fine.

♦ Let go of the circumstances and put your focus on restoring the love and connecting with your life force. Make this your highest priority.

♦ Find the activity that allows you to experience the presence of God. Find what it is and make the connection every day. This is one of the most important things you can do in your life.

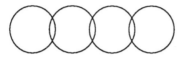

CHAPTER 16

THE CHOICE IS YOURS

There are two different directions to go in life. You can either go for the circumstances or you can go for love.

When your life is about the circumstances, you destroy life. You become full of fear and upset. You become protective and push your dreams away.

When your life is about love, you create life. You become free and alive. You become creative and have your dreams come true.

We have been taught that happiness comes from circumstances, rather than from within. We then spend our lives trying to force the circumstances to be a particular way, thinking this will make us happy, but it never does.

True happiness can only come from within. You create happiness by letting go of your circumstances, bringing forth your love and connecting with your life force.

There comes a point in your personal growth where you get to make a choice. What is your life about? Is your life about forcing the circumstances to be a particular way, or is your life about restoring love?

Regardless of what your life has been about in the past, what is your life going to be about now? Are you committed to the circumstances; or are you committed to a life of love, freedom and inner peace? What is your choice?

As you choose love, you choose life. You also lead the way for those around you to make the same choice. You alter your life and you alter the planet.

Until the world learns to love, there will always be disharmony and suffering. When enough people are willing to take a stand on expressing their love, we will have a world that works. War, crime, hunger and disease will all end. All of life will be an expression of love.

The process of restoring love begins with each one of us. Do what you can to heal your hurt and clean up your life. Be an expression of love and find your way to serve. Connect with your life force.

Miracles are guaranteed.

Thank you and
I love you.

Bill Ferguson

This book is one that you will want to read over and over again. Work with the material and use the book as a reference. Every time you do, you will discover more about yourself and become more effective in your life.

If you are interested in growing more in this area of your life, attend some of our programs and use our books and tapes.

HOW TO HEAL A PAINFUL RELATIONSHIP

*And If Necessary,
How To Part
As Friends*

Paperback, 140 pages

In this unique book, Bill Ferguson shows, step-by-step, how to remove conflict and restore love in any relationship. You will learn what creates love and what destroys it. You will discover how to end the cycle of conflict, release resentment and restore your peace of mind. Bill's experience as a former divorce attorney provides rare insight into the nature of relationships. You will discover something about yourself and your relationships that will alter your life forever.

ISBN 1-878410-00-8 $10

AUDIO AND VIDEO TAPES
TO HELP YOU DISCOVER MORE
ABOUT YOU, YOUR RELATIONSHIPS
AND YOUR LIFE.

ISBN 1-878410-01-6 $65

Set yourself free & enjoy your life

This album includes each of the following 8 audio cassettes for only $65.

Individual cassettes are available for $10, videos for $25.

How To Love Yourself

- Be free of self-invalidation.
- Release the issues that run your life.
- Be able to love yourself just the way you are.

ISBN 1-878410-02-4   Audio $10
ISBN 1-878410-12-1   Video $25

How To Have Love In Your Life

- Discover what creates love.
- Learn why people treat you as they do.
- Have love in all your relationships.

ISBN 1-878410-32-2   Audio $10
ISBN 1-878410-13-X   Video $25

How To Be Free Of Guilt And Resentments

- Be free of all anger, resentment and guilt.
- Restore your inner peace.
- Have difficult relationships work.

ISBN 1-878410-04-0   Audio $10
ISBN 1-878410-14-8   Video $25

How To Be Free Of Upset and Stress

- Be at peace in any circumstance.
- Release the mechanisms that keep you upset.
- Have fear and stress lose their power.

ISBN 1-878410-05-9   Audio $10
ISBN 1-878410-15-6   Video $25

How To Create Prosperity

- Be free of financial stress.
- Discover and release your blocks to prosperity.
- Tap into the natural flow of abundance.

ISBN 1-878410-06-7   Audio $10
ISBN 1-878410-16-4   Video $25

How To Create A Life That Works

- Discover how you create your own unworkability.
- Be free of the hidden actions that sabotage you.
- Learn how to clean up your life.

ISBN 1-878410-07-5   Audio $10
ISBN 1-878410-17-2   Video $25

How To Find Your Purpose

- Earn a living doing what you love.
- Have your life make a difference.
- Discover your life purpose.

ISBN 1-878410-08-3   Audio $10
ISBN 1-878410-18-0   Video $25

How To Experience Your Spirituality

- Connect with your life force.
- Discover God within.
- Experience the Light.

ISBN 1-878410-09-1   Audio $10
ISBN 1-878410-19-9   Video $25

SPIRITUALITY: TEACHINGS FROM A WORLD BEYOND

Two audio cassettes

Several years ago, some profound teachings were received through a form of meditation. Since then, thousands of people have had their lives deeply altered. Through these teachings, you will discover the essence of spirituality. You will experience a oneness with God and will discover a truth that will profoundly alter your life.

ISBN 1-878410-11-3   Audio $18

HOW TO DIVORCE
AS FRIENDS

Two audio cassettes

How you interact with another person determines what happens in your relationship. These audio tapes will show you how to end conflict and adversariness so that your relationship can heal, issues can get resolved, and you can get on with your life. You can be free of the pain and frustration. You will learn how to heal your relationship whether you stay together or not.

ISBN 1-878410-10-5   Audio $18

TO ORDER BOOKS AND TAPES

Item		Price	Qty.	Amount
Miracles Are Guaranteed	Book	$11		
How To Heal A Painful Relationship	Book	$10		
Set Yourself Free Album includes each of the following 8 Audio Cassettes		$65		
• How To Love Yourself	Audio	$10		
	Video	$25		
• How To Have Love In Your Life	Audio	$10		
	Video	$25		
• How To Be Free Of Guilt And Resentment	Audio	$10		
	Video	$25		
• How To Be Free Of Upset And Stress	Audio	$10		
	Video	$25		
• How To Create Prosperity	Audio	$10		
	Video	$25		
• How To Create A Life That Works	Audio	$10		
	Video	$25		
• How To Find Your Purpose	Audio	$10		
	Video	$25		
• How To Experience Your Spirituality	Audio	$10		
	Video	$25		
How To Divorce As Friends 2 Audio Cassettes		$18		
Spirituality: Teachings 2 Audio Cassettes		$18		
			Subtotal	
			Texas residents add 8% sales tax	
			Shipping and handling: Add 10% of Subtotal $2 minimum	
			Total	

Name (Please print) _____

Address _____

City _____

State _____ Zip _____

Telephone   Day (   ) _____   Evening (   ) _____

For MasterCard or Visa orders only:

Card No. _____ Total $ _____

Exp. Date _____   Signature _____

Send your order along with your check or money order to:
Return to the Heart, P.O. Box 541813, Houston, Texas 77254
For Telephone orders Using MasterCard or Visa call (713) 520-5370

TO ORDER BOOKS AND TAPES

Item		Price	Qty.	Amount
Miracles Are Guaranteed	Book	$11		
How To Heal A Painful Relationship	Book	$10		
Set Yourself Free — Album includes each of the following 8 Audio Cassettes		$65		
• How To Love Yourself	Audio	$10		
	Video	$25		
• How To Have Love In Your Life	Audio	$10		
	Video	$25		
• How To Be Free Of Guilt And Resentment	Audio	$10		
	Video	$25		
• How To Be Free Of Upset And Stress	Audio	$10		
	Video	$25		
• How To Create Prosperity	Audio	$10		
	Video	$25		
• How To Create A Life That Works	Audio	$10		
	Video	$25		
• How To Find Your Purpose	Audio	$10		
	Video	$25		
• How To Experience Your Spirituality	Audio	$10		
	Video	$25		
How To Divorce As Friends 2 Audio Cassettes		$18		
Spirituality: Teachings 2 Audio Cassettes		$18		
		Subtotal		
		Texas residents add 8% sales tax		
		Shipping and handling: Add 10% of Subtotal $2 minimum		
		Total		

Name (Please print) _____

Address _____

City _____

State _____   Zip _____

Telephone   Day (   ) _____   Evening (   ) _____

For MasterCard or Visa orders only:

Card No. _____   Total $ _____

Exp. Date _____   Signature _____

Send your order along with your check or money order to:
Return to the Heart, P.O. Box 541813, Houston, Texas 77254
For Telephone orders Using MasterCard or Visa call (713) 520-5370

Let us know if you are interested in:

_____ Having a weekend workshop in your area or traveling to one.

_____ Having a private consulting session on the phone or in person with Bill Ferguson or his staff.

_____ Setting up a radio or television interview with Bill Ferguson.

Call (713) 520-5370 or write to:
Return to the Heart
P.O. Box 541813
Houston, Texas 77254